LEARNING AT BREEZE HILL
1932 - 2012

A Short History of Hillside High School

JOHN PHILLIPS

COUNTYVISE LTD

First Published 2012 by Countyvise Ltd
14 Appin Road, Birkenhead, CH41 9HH

British Library Cataloguing in Publication Data.
A catalogue record for this book is available from the British Library.

ISBN 978 1 906823 75 7

Book and cover design by Charles McIntyre

INTRODUCTION

The idea for this history of Hillside began with the wish to celebrate the 80th anniversary of the opening of the school building on Breeze Hill in 1932, so the pupils have a chance to know more about the history of their school and how education has changed and developed over more than a century. It was so fortunate that one of the best people we could speak to had been to Hillside on a number of occasions and lived "next door" in a block of flats with a wonderful view of the school. Jessie Besford had been present as a pupil at the laying of the foundation stone in 1930 and also the official opening ceremony in 1932. Having found Jessie, I went on to meet other former pupils who shared their memories, photographs and even diaries of their time at school. Sisters Sybil Fraser and Barbara Armitage gave us what at first seemed impossible: a set of written descriptions from letters home to Bootle of life in Herefordshire during evacuation.

It soon became clear that even for a short account, there was a longer history than the one that began in 1932. The girls who moved into the new building at Breeze Hill in 1932 had already been at school in another building – in Balliol Road. Why was a new school building needed? Why build it at Breeze Hill? What was there before? What about the amalgamation with Balliol Secondary School in 1972? On the side of fortune we had records of the schools for girls dating back to before 1910, identifying pupils, teachers and the various curricula in the schools. It was possible to take up the story from the opening of the first school in Balliol Road in 1910, and through trawling through local newspapers and minutes of the Bootle Education Committee bring some life to the documents. Where we lacked fortune was in the absence of records from the Balliol Road Schools for Boys and for Girls, many of them destroyed through vandalism in the 1970s. I would have liked more of the story of those schools, but had already decided that the focus would be on the Breeze Hill site.

It has been possible to take up our story from the opening of the school in Balliol Road in 1910 right through to the present day. I worked at the school for many happy years and I can also remember when it was still a Grammar School for Girls. This book celebrates the history of Hillside and what went before, and also allows us to reflect on wider issues relating to our society that have taken place over that time.

Hillside today caters for all children and provides the right support and inspiration for all. All pupils are individuals and each has their own particular needs: Hillside recognises this and the community of adults working there do their utmost to bring the best out of the children. It has become – as one parent said in sending her son to Breeze Hill – a "truly inclusive school". It has not been easy to achieve this.

I have also tried to provide some food for thought in relating the story of the school to wider issues relating to society. Once a teacher, always a teacher! In order to do this I have included descriptions of some of the earlier teachers associated with the school in order to highlight differences in approaches and attitudes to education and to the teaching profession. It is not easy to build up a picture of teachers from so long ago; however, we can learn from them and I hope these descriptions will prove worthwhile. As I was a teacher at Hillside myself from 1972 until 2011, I have had to decide how best to approach this modern era of the school. It has not been easy, but my own guidelines have been to concentrate on what the school has been like for the pupils whilst mentioning very few by name. I made the same decision about the staff, both teaching and non-teaching, though as the writing took on its own life it became impossible not to mention at least some of them because of their involvement in various aspects of school life. Any ex-pupil reading this account might particularly enjoy remembering some of their teachers; however, I felt I could provide details about teachers from before 1972 but not after.

When I left Hillside in 2011 I retired from a school of which I was extremely proud. Visitors to Hillside always say how impressed they are by the school: the approach and behaviour of the pupils, the smart uniforms, the general calmness in the classrooms, the bright and attractive displays of pupils' work on the walls of classrooms and corridors, and the excellent exam results. This does not "just happen" and that every teacher at Hillside has to work hard both in preparation and in their classroom teaching to make it so. Every year brings its fresh challenges, with some new pupils who do not wish to conform or to meet the challenges they are set. The school is constantly changing in one way or another, but always responding to need and finding the best solutions available. The heart of the school is the pupil, and no one loses sight that Hillside is a child-centred school and that everything is built around them. The staff, both teaching and non-teaching, knows only too well that if they take their eye off the ball for a minute and so there is no complacency.

It is quite wonderful to see what has been accomplished at this school so many years after the opening of the Secondary School for Girls in 1910. It has been a hard road at times, but we should be proud of what we have for the children of the local community at Breeze Hill in 2012 – excellence in the heart of the community.

John Phillips

November 2012

ACKNOWLEDGEMENTS

I began this story with a set of dusty old ledgers and records of the school going back to the early years of the twentieth century. I soon realised that if the story was to be told, it had to begin in 1910 with a building in Balliol Road about which I knew next to nothing. After that, I was able to examine the history of the building at Breeze Hill that was opened in 1932 and today stands proudly as Hillside High School. However, the best part of researching the history of a school is getting to meet former pupils and hearing their stories from years gone by. The school itself has been extremely supportive in helping me put the tale together, especially Ann Henders, Wendy Daly and Neil McCulloch. Laetitia Shemilt was, as ever, an exacting and supportive proof-reader.

Jessie Besford's help was invaluable as she took us back in time and remembered her teachers and friends.

Sybil Fraser, Barbara Armitage and Pat Speak gave me enormous help in piecing together the story of the school evacuation to Kington, providing not only a fascinating insight into life at Hergest Croft but also photographs and written memories from the time.

Anne and Ron Johnson told me some lovely tales and shared photographs.

Marion Hogg shared her memories and photographs from the immediate post-war years.

Jane Rourke, one of the Hillside family, shared her photographs with me.

I enjoyed a lively return to Hillside to show Evelyn Jones, Edna Tritton, Marjorie Sargent and Susan Knight around the school building. They gave a wonderful description of the school as it developed post-war and up until the end of the Grammar School, each of them having been here at a different time and so having different memories. There is still much the former pupils have told me that will have to wait until a fuller version of the story can be produced.

Julia Reid helped me find my way around Kington when I was looking for information and had practically none. Hazel Harvey and Dr. Anne Caunt of Kington shared with me their memories of the evacuation. Mr. and Mrs. Lawrence Banks made me welcome to visit their lovely property of Hergest Croft, whilst family archivist Heather Pegg welcomed me to the building and then showed this "towny" around the beautiful gardens despite the summer showers. I spent so little time in Kington yet learned so much, including the names of the former pupils I then discovered back on Merseyside.

Ex-colleagues Sandie Poole, Ada Jones and John Norton have helped me build a picture of life in the old schools of Balliol Secondary Modern and the Grammar School for Girls. I still meet other ex-colleagues occasionally and if we ever make a larger volume, their memories will be welcomed too.

Andrew Lee-Hart and the team at Sefton Local History Unit and Record Office based at Crosby Library have been of immense help to the school and have made my research easier. Terence Craig helped me learn more about his relative, Ethel Mary Steuart – Head Mistress from 1926 to 1953. Jean Emmerson and Charles McIntyre at Countyvise gave me warm help and support and I learned much from them. Tony Higginson of Formby Bookshop gave me valuable advice about publishing.

Of course I have many memories of my own – I did even attend a Barn Dance at the Grammar School once as well as various school debates when I was a schoolboy myself. I have attempted to be objective in all that I have written, but may have shown my own opinions on the odd occasion. If so, those opinions are mine alone and do not represent the school.

PREFACE

Where does a story begin?

To help us to begin our story, let us look back only a short while to the early years of 2012.

Teijan's mum had worked at Hillside in the school office for a few years and was now returning for a brief visit to see some of her friends there. As they walked down the main drive to the front door the little girl admired the large building built in the early years of the 1930s and was very proud to be going there with her mother. They stepped into the waiting area before being welcomed and allowed to pass through the automatic doors into the foyer. As they waited for her mum's friend to collect them, Teijan looked about her in admiration and smiled. She said, "This was a really beautiful house, Mummy." Her mother smiled at her and said, "Oh, no, Teijan, it wasn't a house. It was built here as a school a long time ago." Teijan insisted she could see the interior of a house and pointed out a lovely staircase to her mum. Her mother's friend had just arrived and heard the conversation. She said, "Well, actually, Teijan has a point because there used to be a house here before the school was built." The child had seen what others do not see – the house that stood on the school site before 1932 and that was named "Markfield" and lived in by the Mather family of Bootle.

So where does our story begin? Let us start with Markfield, the house that stood at the heart of the present-day school, and with Bootle's need for a new school for girls in the early 20th century that led eventually to the school we all know today.

THE MATHER FAMILY AND MARKFIELD HOUSE

Neither John Philips Mather nor any of his family ever saw the school that was built on Breeze Hill, but they did play a part in the story as a whole. He had been born in the final years of the 18th century. He made his fortune in Liverpool as an Iron Merchant, and brought up his family of nine children in the district of Everton, near to St. George's Church (known locally as the "cast-iron church" because of its iron interiors and roof). As Liverpool grew and more people moved into this area, Mather moved his family in the mid-19th century to a very tranquil and rural area near to the river – Bootle. He bought Bootle Hall, previously owned by the Irlam family, and the largest freehold property in Bootle at the time. Mather had become a very rich and influential man and employed five servants. His family consisted of six daughters: Sophia, Elizabeth, Fanny, Clara, Julia, Susan; and sons Frank, George and Herbert.

Gradually, the working population of Bootle grew also, particularly because of the development of the docks from Liverpool into Bootle. The town had been a village in 1821 with a population of 808. This had grown to 4,106 in 1851 and 27,112 in 1881. Between 1859 and 1881, Canada Dock, Brocklebank Dock, Langton Dock and Alexandra Dock were all opened. Bootle Hall was no longer in such a quiet area with the building of houses for the workers, warehouses and the opening of trade suppliers in the area. In 1868 Bootle became a Borough Corporate. Bootle was a town, growing fast, and it was time for the Mathers to move home again.

Before they moved, John Philips Mather had given the sum of £8000 to build Christ Church in Bootle: with the growing population of the Borough, a new church was badly needed. Mather, however, had another reason for endowing the new church: it was meant as a memorial to his youngest daughter Susan Harriet Mather, who had died aged sixteen in 1864. Two years later the church was complete and was opened by the Bishop of Chester. It was faced in red sandstone, probably taken from Woolton Quarry from where the stone used for Liverpool Cathedral originated. The Liverpool Echo reported that it was "a large and handsome building, and is erected upon a commanding site at the top of Merton-road, in the village of Bootle." You will still find J.P.Mather's name inside the church today.

The church remained within the hands and "perpetual right of patronage" of the Mather family until 1920 when the three living sons of John Philips Mather agreed to turn this over to the Bishop of Liverpool. We can begin to grasp the wealth and influence of the Mathers if we look at their positions in society at this time. The Reverend Frank Albert Mather and the Right Reverend Bishop Herbert Mather had built careers within the Church and Arthur Stanley Mather C.B.E was a well-known solicitor in Woolton.

When the Mather family moved again, they remained in Bootle but this time had a house built on undeveloped land just beyond the new church, on Breeze Hill. This house was named "Markfield" and by 1881 they were living there with a staff of six servants: housekeeper, lady's maid, parlour maid, upper house maid, middle house maid, kitchen maid and general maid. These servants came from across the UK, but none were from Bootle. This was a prime area to live for the wealthy of Bootle and remained so for many years. To one side of Markfield was another large house, occupied by a steam ship owner; on the side that borders Stuart Road was Stuart College, a small school run by a Welsh graduate of Oxford University. Markfield was the final home of the Mathers. John Philips Mather died in 1884, his wife Elizabeth in 1898 aged 97, his daughter Fanny died the same year aged 66, and Julia died in 1904 aged 59. The final daughter to die was Clara in 1916 aged 83, still being looked after by a team of five servants. The family were all buried near to their original home at St. George's Church. Yet when little Teijan visited the school, she could sense what had been there when the Mathers occupied the house and in her own eyes could see something of what the house had been like.

After that, the house lay empty. However, the land itself was actually owned by the Earl of Derby, and in only a few years he would have reason to sell the land and houses over to Bootle Council. This would provide the opportunity to build a new school for Bootle in 1932.

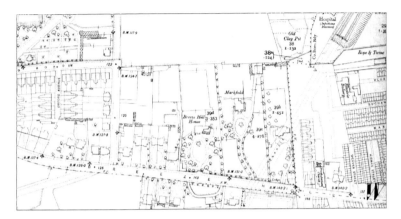

This excerpt from the 1908 Ordnance Survey map shows the site when Markfield still stood and Miss Clara Mather was still resident there. The school was built on the land containing Breeze Hill House, Markfield and Stuart College.

- The houses on the other side of Breeze Hill House were demolished to construct Southport Road and Fernhill Road at about the same time as our school was built.

- Stuart College runs along Stuart Road and we can identify where the building actually stood by comparing its situation with the houses on the other side of Stuart Road and which are still standing in 2012.

We can all recognise from this map from over a hundred years ago that Bootle was a different place. Life simply doesn't stand still and each generation is different. Then, there were more horses and carts than cars, many trams, thoroughly different clothes – just find some books of old photographs of the town and you will begin to see the differences. When you see those faces from our past looking at the camera or simply walking by on their everyday business, remember that they were real people – as real as you and me – with family, friends, jobs, hopes, dreams, cares, worries, and so much life to lead. Imagine the tramcars and buses travelling noisily along the roads, the many small shops selling different goods and the children going to and from school on weekdays; you will begin to help the words and illustrations in this small book become an active remembrance of people living at another time and who might very well include family of yours from what was not really so long ago. Use your imagination and make the story come alive!

CHAPTER 1 – 1910-32

The First Secondary School for Girls in Bootle

Hillside High School's history can be traced back to 1910 when "Bootle Secondary School for Girls" was established in a new building for 200 pupils in Balliol Road, on a site between the old Secondary School for Boys and the Public Swimming Baths. The first Head was Miss Lydia Taylor. Under her leadership the numbers of the school grew rapidly. Three new buildings had to be purchased by Bootle Council to deal with this, but it was clear that eventually a brand new school would need to be built. The school's second Head was Dr. E.M. Steuart, who took over in 1926. In the late 1920s Bootle Council found their solution for a new school and planned for it to be built on the site of our Hillside High School for use by pupils in 1931, later pushed back to 1932. Outside the main entrance to Hillside we can still see the Foundation Stone laid in 1930 and the stone commemorating the school's opening in 1932.

Bootle today lies within the Metropolitan District of Sefton in Merseyside. It lies just to the north of Liverpool, and Hillside High School lies on the border between Sefton and Liverpool, marked by Breeze Hill and Stuart Road. Bootle became a County Borough in 1889, separated from Lancashire. In 1903 there was a strong move to absorb Bootle into Liverpool but this was resisted and Bottle remained a self-governing unit until the reorganisation of local government in 1974 upon which it became part of Sefton.

The forerunner of Hillside High School was Bootle Secondary School for Girls (BSSG), opened in Balliol Road in 1910. If we want to understand Hillside's history and the reason why a school was built at Breeze Hill in 1932, we have to start here. First, we should try to understand what was different about this school from the other schools in Bootle and why it was so important for Bootle Council to build it. Any pupil who had any thought of moving on to a university or a college at this time had to go to a school set up to prepare them to do so. In 1905 there wasn't a Secondary School for Girls, though there did exist one for boys. Virtually all pupils went to an Elementary School until they were 14 and then they left to work or live with their parents. The Elementary Schools were free to all children.

A Secondary School was different. They had a four-year curriculum leading to examinations in English language and literature, geography, history, a foreign language, mathematics, science, drawing, manual work, physical training, and, for girls, housewifery. These schools had to have an "academic bias" and would be the path to further education for their pupils. One other factor we should understand is that in many cases parents had to pay fees for their children to go to a Secondary School. We know that today it is free for all pupils to go to school until the age of 18 unless they go to a private school, where fees must be paid. In 1907 a system of "free places" - the free place scholarship system – were introduced to give children in Elementary Schools who showed academic promise the opportunity to go to a Secondary School. Children would take an examination at the age of eleven and those who "passed" were given a place at the Secondary School, which was obliged to admit "free place scholars" who had spent at least two years at a Public Elementary School. Parents had to pay fees varying between £2 per term for Bootle children and £2-7 shillings per term for those living outside. It doesn't seem much in modern-day money, but it was a real commitment for many parents at that time. The free places were later known as "special places", and it was not until the 1944 Education Act that fees for secondary schools were abolished altogether.

At the start of the twentieth century, Bootle Council was attempting to create a system of education that would meet the needs of all the children of the borough. They were desperately keen to have Secondary Schools for both boys and girls. The school for boys evolved from the Technical School in Balliol Road; the Council decided in 1905 that they had to find a site for a school for girls and build it as soon as possible.

In 1910 the Education Committee opened a Secondary School for Girls for 200 scholars – Bootle Secondary School for Girls. It was opened on the small site of what had previously been "Balliol Gardens", between the Technical School and the Swimming Baths. The Technical School was later known as the Boys' Secondary School. Today, both of these buildings have been demolished and redeveloped by Hugh Baird College.

Girls' Secondary School, Balliol Road, Bootle: Opened September 1910

The *Bootle Times* gave a full report of the ceremony of opening the new school in Balliol Road in 1910 as well as of the speeches made. The chief guest on the day was Sir Benjamin Johnson, the founder and owner of Johnsons the Cleaners. Sir Ben had only just received a knighthood from the King.

The new building contained eight classrooms, one laboratory, one art room and an assembly hall. There was no dining room or cookery room; however, the girls were able to use the facilities of the Boys' School next door. Gym was taught either in the Baths on the other side of the new

On this Ordnance Survey map from 1908 we can see the Municipal Technical School (later the Boys' Secondary School) and the Public Baths. Lying between them is a garden area, Balliol Road Gardens, upon which the Girls' Secondary School was built.

building (with the pool boarded over) or in the yard at the rear of the building. Though designed for 200 girls, it soon became clear that this was not enough and three houses had to be used for the growing numbers of pupils. The size of the school soon grew to 334 scholars. The cost had been £6,800.

Bootle Secondary School for Girls 1910 - 1932

The first Headmistress was Miss Lydia Taylor M.A., who called it a "beautiful building" during her speech at the Opening. She told her audience that children's development was largely through the medium of books and she asked parents to join with the teachers in helping to provide more books for the children and please not to grumble at the bills. She added that the aim of the school was to send out girls who would prove to be able to take their places as strong, pure-minded women, whether as teachers, business-women or women in the home. The Senior Mistress was Helen Hunter M.A. from Edinburgh, and another teacher who played a vital role in the development of the school was Gwladys Williams from Bangor, North Wales. There was clearly much drive and dedication to get the school up and running, from the children aged between 5 and 11 in the Preparatory Section to the older pupils aged 11 to 18 in the Secondary School proper.

In 1910 the subjects in the Secondary curriculum were English, Latin, Science, Geography, French, Mathematics, Drawing, Music, Domestic Subjects and Physical Exercises. In 1912 Needlework replaced Domestic Subjects.

> Forms I and II comprised the Preparatory Sections.
>
> The Secondary school began with pupils aged 11 in either Form Upper III or Lower III.
>
> Lower Remove and IV were for pupils aged 12-13. They were known as the "Second Year".
>
> Third Year was Upper IV.
>
> Fourth Year was Form V.

Pupils at the school could leave at the age of 15. Those who stayed on would go into the Upper Vth and the VIth Form. They would study for a "Preliminary Certificate" and "Matriculation". Today, the best known qualifications in secondary schools as of 2012-13 are GCSEs, BTECs and, for some, the Baccalaureate. Until 1917 there was no recognised national certificate for pupils to achieve. Eventually, the Government set up two standard examinations: School Certificate at 16 and Higher School Certificate at 18. For the School Certificate it was necessary to pass English and four other subjects: pupils had a certain amount of choice in these other subjects. This remained the key qualification until the introduction of the GCEs in 1951.

The school ran a prefect system and appointed a Head Girl each year. The girls chosen as prefects were given much responsibility and this carried on right into the 1960s. In the lovely photograph opposite, discovered by Barbara Armitage in a car boot sale, we can see the prefects from 1921-22.

Seated in the centre is Head Girl Dilys Blyde, who later returned to the Grammar School as Headmistress in 1953. The other prefects are, running clockwise, Daisy Grindley, Marion Brown, Grace Wilson, Helena Sace, Muriel Griffiths, Elsie Ball and Edna Simms.

The Search for a Larger Building

Towards the end of World War I, the number of fee-paying scholars increased and from an original intake of 200 pupils the number had grown in 1919 to 334! Three nearby houses had been bought to provide extra accommodation, but this was not a satisfactory state of affairs. Throughout the 1920s Bootle Council looked at ways of providing a new building for the girls.

There was little free land left available in Bootle on which to build a new school, but an opportunity to do so came through the Earl of Derby, the principal landowner in Bootle (Derby Park, Derby Road and Stanley Road were all named after the family) and who had been involved with the opening of the school in 1910. Remember that the land that the house "Markfield" was built upon actually was owned by the Lord Derby. He offered Bootle this land for the "relatively small sum" of £10,500; he believed it was a fine site for a new school building that would be a flagship for education in the borough. It was agreed that this was a very handsome gift to the Bootle community.

However, the purchase of the land and the need to move to a new building was not enough to ensure that it all actually transpired: the money would have to be found to pay for the new building, and not all councillors were able to agree that this was the most appropriate way to use taxpayers' money. Whilst the politicians argued, the grounds on Markfield were allowed to be used by the Girl Guides, for Christ Church pupils and a number of events such as the Juvenile Empire Day Festival of 1926. The building of a new school was put off again when the Council agreed to lay out the grounds at Breeze Hill as playing fields for both of the two Secondary Schools. By 1927 they were looking to create three football pitches, eight tennis courts and one hockey pitch, with the existing stables modified for use as changing rooms and as many of the existing trees as possible to be preserved, as well as any shrubberies. They returned to the scheme in March 1928 when an architect was asked to submit two plans, one incorporating the two existing houses and the other for an entirely new build. On reviewing his ideas, the Education Committee decided upon the new build and approved his plans in March 1929. The original opening date of September 1931 had to be postponed owing to building delays. It was eventually opened, fully-equipped as a school, at Easter 1932.

Here is a picture from the *Bootle Times* in July 1929 showing the Girls' Secondary School Sports. It was held on a Saturday afternoon and so a large number of parents were able to attend.

You can see the Championship Shields that were presented to the winning Forms: Upper Vb, Upper IVb and IIIa. Each winner received a brooch as did the second-placed girls. The brooches had been designed by some of the senior girls and enamelled in the school colours, winners' names in gold and runners-up in silver.

Lydia Taylor remained as Head of what Bootle Education Committee believed was an excellent and successful school. Sadly, after suffering for some time with ill health, she died in 1926. During her illness, Helen Hunter acted in her place. In 1926 a new Headmistress was appointed: Dr. Ethel M. Steuart, a classical scholar and fellow of Girton College, Oxford. Helen Hunter herself died at a relatively early age in 1929 and was succeeded as Senior Mistress by Mary Mercer from Bootle. Gwladys Williams, remembered today through her annual prize for Character and Personality in school, remained as the senior English mistress until her retirement in 1942.

There was a very great difference in school life and teaching styles from what we know today. Lydia Taylor had been highly qualified, but had a particular passion for self-improvement, raising educational opportunities for girls and challenging them to make their way in the world. Ethel Steuart was a highly-regarded classical scholar and academic whose two previous posts had been in Classics departments at universities. She did have one term's previous experience at her old school and had taken a course in education, but her appointment was made more upon her national standing as an expert in Latin and Greek and the strength of her academic qualifications than on experience in secondary education. It is fair to say that all the candidates for the Headship in 1926 were very highly qualified, but none as much as Dr. Steuart.

She made some changes to BSSG's curriculum, including adding the option of studying Greek for some girls in Form VI. In the 1928 syllabus, Domestic Subjects returned, and Drawing, Singing and Elocution were added. Dr. Steuart taught a group of ten students Greek with her in her first year. One other innovation was that of the annual prize giving evening at Speech Day, which became an important fixture in school life. Indeed, it remains so today as "Presentation Evening" and is an absolute highlight of the year, celebrating the work of the pupils as well as the quality of their performance in music, song and dance.

SOME TEACHERS FROM THE PAST

It is easy to think that because something happened so long ago then it cannot be important for us today. However, that is not true. Whatever we are today has been built upon what was done in the past and what we have learned from it. It is when we ignore the lessons of the past that we make mistakes.

We don't know much about the teachers from the past so it would be easy to generalise about them and assume they were all the same. But they weren't all the same! Just like today's teachers, they were different individuals with different backgrounds, ideas, characters and different abilities to work with the pupils and get the best from them. Yes, they were different to teachers today because the times were different: they wore different styles of clothing; mostly they were unmarried women who were always called the "Mistresses" by the pupils. Their training was different and their teaching far more formal. Apart from the war years, they taught only girls after the age of 11 right up until the opening of Hillside in 1972.

We have extremely few photos of teachers before WWII, and what we do know is mainly gleaned from old newspaper reports, old school records and, rarely now, the memories of some pupils. Of the four people described here, only Dr. Steuart is still remembered by many pupils – she left the school in 1953. Only two could recall Miss Williams, and none can remember Lydia Taylor or Helen Hunter. Make no mistake, however: in their different ways, each of these former teachers had an influence on the school, the pupils and the Bootle community.

LYDIA TAYLOR – FIRST HEADMISTRESS
1910-1926

Lydia Taylor was born into a Quaker family in Macclesfield in 1874. She went to school in a Quaker boarding school in Ackworth, near Wakefield in Yorkshire. She took a B.A. at Owens College in Manchester in 1894 and went straight into the teaching profession as an Assistant Mistress at her old school. She returned to Owens College in 1897 for a year to take an M.A. in Latin and French. Academic qualifications were extremely important for teachers at this time, especially for anyone with aspirations to be a Head teacher. Lydia then did what many young women did after leaving university: she travelled in Europe for a year or so, developing their ability to speak foreign languages (usually French and German, and possibly Italian) and steeping themselves in the cultures of those countries. She was a teacher for the first five years of the 20th century in York at the Mount School before moving to Haslemere in Surrey as Joint Principal. Clearly she had ideas about teaching and had ambitions of becoming a Head. In order to attain her dream she went to the Manchester Training Department in 1909 and took a Diploma Class I in Education. She could now apply for a job that would enable her to develop her beliefs in a school – and in 1910 she was successful in her application to become the first Head Mistress of the brand new Secondary School for Girls in Balliol Road, Bootle.

Her job was to establish the school, build up the numbers of pupils, ensure a high quality of teaching and raise the aspirations of the Bootle girls who attended the school. There is little evidence that remains today of her work at the school, other than occasional references to her in the minutes of the Education Committee and her eventual obituary in the *Bootle Times*. Yet that is enough to inform us that Lydia Taylor was held in the highest esteem by the local Councillors and her colleagues in school and was clearly a strong-minded person who knew the immense value of a good education to the girls in Bootle at this time. She dedicated her life to her school and her pupils, living the

A LADY OF NOBLE CHARACTER.

TRIBUTES TO THE LATE MISS LYDIA TAYLOR, M.A.

FIRST HEADMISTRESS OF SECONDARY SCHOOL.

Great regret has been occasioned by the news of the death of Miss Lydia Taylor, M.A., head mistress of the Bootle Secondary School for Girls. Miss Taylor, who passed away in Middleton, near Manchester, on Monday, had been in a feeble state of health for many months, and in view of this resigned her appointment, which would have terminated at the end of the present term.

The Secondary School for Girls was opened in September, 1910, and Miss Taylor was selected as the head mistress from a number of highly qualified applicants. She came to Bootle with high credentials, and after having had valuable experience in other secondary schools.

The establishment of a new school is always an onerous and responsible duty, but Miss Taylor showed that she possessed considerable powers of organisation. In a short time the school was filled, and soon took its place among the schools of higher education in the district. The original premises provided accommodation for about 200 girls, but so rapidly were the places filled, and such was the demand for further accommodation, that the Education Committee acquired adjacent premises and were enabled to provide for some 350 scholars. The school became noted for its high scholastic standard, as well as for its admirable tone and discipline, and it has always received excellent reports from H.M. Inspectors.

whole time in the second floor of a house in Trinity Road, owned by Bootle Council and situated next door to the Town Hall.

She was Head from 1910 up until 1926, and in that time the local Council was extremely proud of BSSG. Lydia began to suffer illness in the mid-1920s and eventually had to leave her post in the hands of her Assistant to return to her family home in Oldham in November 1925 to try to recover. Eventually, she died in April the following year aged only 52 and was buried in the local Quaker church. She received the warmest and most glowing tributes from members of the Council and her colleagues at school. There is no doubt that what we do know about Lydia Taylor is that she established the Secondary School from its first day and for the next sixteen years till 1926. The people in her own time who did know her, valued her and loved her. That tells us what we need to know.

HELEN HUNTER – SECOND MISTRESS
(DEPUTY HEAD) 1910-1929

Helen Anderson Hunter was nine years younger than Lydia Taylor and born in Scotland in April 1883.

Her father was a schoolmaster who moved to Edinburgh with his family a few years later when he became the Head of a boarding school. They lived near the university in 17 West Savile Terrace, which remained the family home after Helen had moved to Bootle. Helen was educated at the well-known George Watson's Ladies College in Edinburgh before taking an M.A. in French and Latin at Edinburgh University. She began to show her interest in education as a career when she studied at St. George's Training College in the same year as she finished her M.A. She attained other diplomas in education at Cambridge and Edinburgh before travelling through France and Germany when she was 22 – 23. She studied in Paris to be awarded the Diplôme Supérieur de l'Alliance Française in Paris. She then taught for four years at the Girls' High School in Halifax, Yorkshire, before moving to Bootle in 1910 as Assistant Mistress to Lydia Taylor. They worked together to develop the team of teachers at BSSG, a key member of the team being Gwladys Williams. Helen was another career teacher and shared the second floor apartment with her Head until Lydia Taylor's death. In those very difficult years when Lydia was suffering from pernicious anaemia, Helen not only held the reins at the school as Acting Headmistress but she also did her utmost to try to support Lydia and nurse her through her illness.

When Lydia Taylor died, Helen reverted to being Assistant Mistress and supported Ethel Steuart in her early years as Head. She moved out of Trinity Road and went to Burscough to share a house in the countryside though very close to Ormskirk with her friend and colleague Gwladys Williams. It was a lovely place to live, very close to Aughton Park station and a train line to Bootle.

Sadly, Helen had her own health problems and died in July 1929, aged only 46. The Education Committee had already praised her major contributions to the school in 1926, and at her death they were equally grateful and fulsome. She was buried in Kirkdale cemetery.

In the summer 1930 School Newsletter, senior pupils paid tribute to her as a person and a teacher.

A NOBLE WOMAN.

DEATH OF MISS H. A. HUNTER, OF GIRLS' SECONDARY SCHOOL.

The news of the passing of Miss Helen A. Hunter, M.A., who has been for many years an assistant mistress at the Bootle Secondary School for Girls, and who, in latter years, occupied the important position of second mistress, will be received with much regret in the Borough. Miss Hunter had been in very indifferent health for some months, and, following operations at the David Lewis Northern Hospital, her death occurred on Tuesday evening.

As a teacher of many excellent qualifications, and as a woman of outstanding personality, Miss Hunter will be long remembered by a very wide circle of friends and pupils and former pupils. During her 19 years' service in Bootle, hundreds of girls have passed through her hands and it is not an exaggeration to say that they bear the imprint of her influence and character. By the scholars she was beloved and the staff held her in the highest esteem. The Education Committee have lost a mistress of wide scholarship and of extraordinary teaching ability.

"The passing of such a noble woman at the zenith of her powers is, indeed, distressing, and her demise is greatly regretted by educational circles in Bootle," writes a correspondent. "Her deep devotion to the late headmistress (Miss Taylor) in her long illness was only characteristic of Miss Hunter's unselfish and generous nature."

The funeral is at Kirkdale Cemetery to-day (Friday), at 11 a.m.

"The Mistresses know best of Miss Hunter's work as Second Mistress and as an Acting Headmistress; we know of her as a teacher and a Form Mistress. There must be a great number of girls, past and present, who can testify wholeheartedly to the value of Miss Hunter's work as teacher. Her subjects were French and Latin, and we know how careful and scholarly her teaching was in both these subjects; often we hardly realised that there were any difficulties, and they were made so easy for us by the patient preparation which led up to them. How many, too, were the extra lessons given to help us! We are glad to hear that one of Miss Hunter's past girls has gained a Double First Class Degree in French at Liverpool University.

"Those of us who had the privilege of having Miss Hunter as a Form Mistress are beginning to realise how much we were to her. She knew when to praise, when to blame, when to encourage, and when to "blaze." She knew all our weaknesses and when we needed help, we knew that she would not fail us. We cannot express our loving appreciation of her care for us.

"But we have not said all when we say that Miss Hunter was a great teacher and a fine Form Mistress. She was a friend to us – her gaiety, her sense of fun brought us into a closer touch with her. She made us realise that schoolgirls need something in addition to work, and broadened our vision, so that we began to realise something of the true meaning of life. "

The girls then set about raising funds through a number of activities to set up the H.A.Hunter Memorial Fund. This included "Miss Williams' Concerts" and "Miss Benson's Crossword Puzzle Competition, a "Nursery Rhyme Fair" and an evening of entertainment. "The day was even more successful than was anticipated, over £100 being realised." That was a large amount of money for 1930. "This was partly due to the so gladly given work of the Mistresses and girls, but chiefly to the tireless efforts of Miss Williams, who supervised and advised the girls."

GWLADYS WILLIAMS – HEAD OF ENGLISH

1910-1942

We have already come across Gwladys Williams in the mini-biographies of the previous two teachers. She was born in Prince's Road, Bangor, North Wales, in November 1882, just one year older than Helen Hunter. She had two sisters. She was a pupil at Bangor County School for Girls before going to The University of Wales at Bangor where she achieved a First in Education, Philosophy and English in 1905. She travelled to Leeds for her first teaching post and, two years later, went to Bootle to join the Pupil-Teacher Centre in Balliol Road. This ceased to exist in 1910 when the new Secondary School was opened, and Gwladys joined Lydia and Helen in the new enterprise.

Gwladys lived in various flats and houses over the years, mainly travelling to school by various trams, trains and buses. She was not far away from her family home and kept in touch with them. She was sharing a house in Harlech Road near the Blundellsands station at the time she retired. Jessie Besford remembered her as an excellent teacher with a sharp sense of humour; Barbara Shepherd remembered her teaching English in what is now room 3 at Hillside, though in those days the teachers moved rooms and it was the pupils who generally stayed in one base. She was a short lady, about 5 feet in height, who liked wearing darker clothes. She clearly loved music and took pupils to concerts in Liverpool. In the 1930 school magazine there is an article written by "Sir Beecham Pill" (a play on words based on a famous conductor Sir Thomas Beecham and a well-known laxative of the day, invented by Beecham's grandfather, the Beecham Pill). If anyone wrote that article it was Gwladys Williams with her deep love and understanding of music and her sharp sense of humour. "Describing a visit to the Picton Hall, the author concluded: "We left the Hall regretfully, "andantino", but the following season we hope to return "molto allegro"".

Gwladys Williams worked through WWI and eventually retired at the age of 60 in 1942, during WWII. With many of the school away due to evacuation at the time, she enjoyed working with boys as well as girls in her final year as the pupils remaining in Bootle were mixed together at Breeze Hill. It was a challenge for everyone, but gradually everyone got used to the idea and the school settled down. At the end of her career, she agreed to stay on for one more term to help out at a time when it was very difficult to find teachers – many men were in the armed forces, many teachers were away with the evacuated children, and Bootle was a dangerous place to be following the notorious May Blitz. In December 1942 she did finish and was given a lovely Reception in the Hall at Breeze Hill. In attendance were scholars past and present, the staff, Director of Education Warwick Bolam and representatives of Bootle Council and the Mayor and Mayoress. Mayoress Miss E. Jones was an ex-pupil and said that Gwladys had two outstanding qualities: her sense of humour and her fairness. She added that, "As long as Miss Williams was looking after the English side of things , we felt we were safe." Gwladys thanked the audience and told them a few stories about her career. She concluded with the words, "This evening teems with memories for me. And now I have another precious one which will bring me happiness in the future – the memory of your great kindness and regard."

Sadly, she had virtually no time to enjoy her well-earned retirement. Only two days later she suffered a cerebral hemorrhage, having suffered from high blood pressure for some while. She never recovered.

Gladys Williams is still remembered at Hillside today through the Prizes for Character and Personality that were named after her after the War and which are awarded each year at Presentation Evening.

Sudden Death of Miss G. Williams

Two Days after Receiving Presentation

TWO days after receiving a retiring testimonial from the school where she had laboured faithfully for 34 years, Miss Gwladys Williams, former English mistress of Bootle Secondary School for Girls, died on Friday evening, following a seizure.

Miss Williams, through whose hands generations of Bootle girls had passed, was one of the most popular mistresses in Bootle, and was held in affectionate esteem by literally thousands of her former pupils.

Having reached the age of sixty years, she retired at the end of the summer term, but had given further service to the school during the autumn term.

Last Wednesday a gathering representative of past and present scholars of the Girls' Secondary School and staff assembled to testify their appreciation of Miss Williams on her retirement, and presented to her a beautiful silver tea service. The hope was expressed that she would enjoy a long and happy retirement. Two days later she had a seizure and was rushed to Waterloo Hospital, but her death had taken place before further aid could be rendered.

Miss Williams was living with a niece at Blundellsands. Her sisters live at Bangor, North Wales, and a cousin is Matron of the Liverpool Radium Institute.

The funeral took place yesterday (Wednesday) at Bangor, and simultaneously a memorial service was held at the Girls' Secondary School, conducted by the Rev. Canon E. Mayson, Vicar of Christ Church.

THE PRESENTATION

At the presentation to Miss Williams last week the Mayor (Alderman R. O. Jones) presided, and was accompanied by the Mayoress (Miss K. Jones, B.A.) who

liams had been an excellent mistress. Miss Williams had won the love, affection and esteem of the staff, scholars and the Education Committee from the Director downwards.

The Mayoress (Miss K. Jones, B.A.) recalled that it was 28 years since she first met Miss Williams. Her two outstanding qualities were her sense of humour and her fairness. Recalling her own school life under the tuition of Miss Williams, the Mayoress said, "As long as Miss Williams was looking after the English side of things, we felt we were safe." She concluded by thanking Miss Williams for the work she had done for the Borough.

Mr. W. H. Bolam, Director of Education, said he felt sure that Miss Williams would have happy memories of the school, and would still take an active interest in its work.

Miss M. Mercer (acting headmistress) said she had known Miss Williams for a

LAST WORDS

"THIS evening teems with memories for me. And now I have another precious one which will bring me happiness in the future—the memory of your great kindness and regard."

The closing sentence of Miss Williams' speech at the Girls' Secondary School presentation last week.

great number of years, and was one of her oldest friends. Her duty was to speak on behalf of the staff. After tracing some of the history of the school, Miss Mercer conveyed very best wishes to Miss Williams and expressed the hope that she would have a happy and long retirement.

MISS WILLIAMS' REPLY

In her reply Miss Williams said: I should like to say how glad I am that the boys and girls in school last year have shared in this presentation. I consider that last year was a very special one, because it marked the first dual school in Bootle. It was difficult for masters and mistresses, as we had to change our methods. Some pupils who came to school had no intention of doing any work; the staff were determined that they were

gether and I have already realised how much I miss the friendship and companionship of the staff and girls. She asked for her thanks to be conveyed to the parents at Southport (under Miss Walkers) for their share in the gift, and also the girls in Herefordshire. She was glad to see such a representative gathering of old girls especially, as she realised that they had very little leisure time.

MOTHERS AND DAUGHTERS

Miss Williams remarked that there were few daughters present who had seen her pupils. When a daughter followed a mother, it gave her particular satisfaction.

Miss Williams then spoke of the pleasure experienced by mistresses and girls when they first came to the new building, and how they enjoyed the peaceful surroundings after the roar of traffic and the nearness to which they had become accustomed in their old school in Balliol Road. She hoped present scholars were as grateful as the first users, and that they would not take the school for granted, as it was a building to be proud of.

In a flash of humour Miss Williams added, "I must not forget the old boys whom I have taught—or at least tried to."

EDUCATION COMMITTEE TRIBUTE

Tribute was paid to Miss G. Williams by members of the Bootle Education Committee at their meeting on Thursday of last week, the day before her death.

At a meeting of the Higher Education Committee, the Mayor, Alderman R. O. Jones, said that Miss Williams served for thirty-seven years as English mistress and had done exceedingly good work. He thought it would be wise and prudent, on behalf of the Education Committee, to thank her for her services, and express the desire that she should enjoy good health and long retirement.

Councillor C. A. Rogers, Alderman Mrs. E. J. Smith and Alderman R. J. Rainford joined in the tributes.

NAVAL CADETSHIPS

Applications to attend the February, 1929, examination for Naval Cadetships at the Royal Naval College, Dartmouth, must be received by the Secretary of the Admiralty (C. W. Branch) not later than the 10th January, 1949.

Applications can only be considered from candidates born on between 1st August, 1929, and 30th November, 1929. The educational test to be undertaken by candidates is the Common Examination for entrance to Public Schools.

In addition to the ordinary entry ten scholarships are offered for competition at each examination to boys from Grant and Secondary Schools, and up to ten to boys from other schools. Generous financial

Miss G. Williams

DR. E.M.STEUART – HEADMISTRESS
1926-1953

Ethel Mary Steuart, MA, DLitt., was the second headmistress of BSSG and a long-serving member of the teaching staff. She was the product of an academic and financially comfortable family around the turn of the 20th century. She remained an academic in outlook and temperament throughout her life.

Her father was John Alexander Steuart, a novelist and journalist, and her mother Annie Maude Craig from Coleraine, Northern Ireland. Ethel was born in 1888 and went to school at the North London Collegiate School, for which she won the Clothworkers' Scholarship. Her ability in gaining that scholarship can be matched throughout the rest of her formal education – she was a highly able and academic person. It is also possible to realise why Ethel would later take on the role of Head Mistress in Bootle, despite starting her working life in universities. The influence that her school had on her during her time there between 1899 and 1908 must have been very strong and stimulated her immensely through her formative years.

The Head Mistress during Ethel's time was another leading feminist and active suffragist, Sophie Bryant. Mrs. Bryant was well-known in her time on many fronts, not the least as a pioneer in education for women, and was one of the first women to obtain a 1st class honours degree in Science when the University of London opened its degree courses to women in 1881. She was also the first woman to receive a Doctorate in Science in England, yet also found time for travels abroad and climbed both the Matterhorn and Mont Blanc as well as being credited by many people as having been one of the first women in the UK to own and ride a bicycle! Sophie Bryant had an immense influence as a teacher and educationalist, an influence that would have had a great impact on Ethel as well as others of her generation who became teachers and Heads.

Ethel went on to University College, London where she was awarded a B.A (Honours) class 1 in Classics. She then went to Girton College, Cambridge, to read Classics and during her four years there she was awarded the Gamble Prize, a Research Studentship and was made a Fellow of the College. Ethel sat the Classical Tripos Cambridge (Honours Examination) and was awarded Part I Class 1 in 1911 and Part II Class I in 1912. She continued her studies in 1912-13 at Berlin University, Paris and the British School of Archaeology in Rome to undertake research for a thesis for which she was awarded an MA at London.

She began to develop her interest in education by training at the Maria Grey Training College (University of London) 1913-1914, achieving the University Diploma in Pedagogy with Distinction. This college had been created in the 19th century by the Women's Education Union to promote women's right to education and the professional recognition of women teachers.

The choice facing Ethel was whether to follow the path into education in secondary schools or in universities. In September 1914, just two months into the First World War, she took employment for a term as classical mistress at her old secondary school. She then took an academic role as Assistant lecturer in Latin at University College, Cardiff. She remained there for all but the last month of the war before moving to Edinburgh University in October 1918 as Assistant to the Professor of Latin, becoming Lecturer in Latin herself in June 1921. When she moved to Edinburgh from London, her parents joined her; her brother was living in nearby Renfrewshire, too.

This was Ethel's preparation for becoming Head Mistress of a Secondary School for Girls in 1926. She applied for the post in the spring of 1926 following the early death of Lydia Taylor. She was successful against five other candidates, all with strong academic credentials, though none as strong as Ethel's. We can learn so much about secondary education in the first half of the 20th century through our analysis of her preparation for the role of Head Mistress. She had taken a two-year course it a college of education and had spent one term teaching classics at her old school. That, plus eleven years working in universities, was her preparation to lead a school. Lydia Taylor's career had been more directly built around education, although based upon strong academic ability and success. When she moved to Bootle to live at 8 Oxford Road, a large house that was close to the site of what became the new school in 1932, she moved once again with her parents and the family maid, Minnie.

In her first year in charge she instituted an annual prize giving ceremony, generally known as "Speech Night": it was held traditionally on the final Friday in November with a guest speaker to present the prizes. It was invariably reported fully in the *Bootle Times* as the BSSG was seen, together with the Secondary School for Boys, as the premier

schools in Bootle. Initially they were held at the Town Hall in Bootle, later transferring in 1932 to Breeze Hill and the new school building. For the first Speech Night, the new Vice-Chancellor of Liverpool University was invited. One of the most impressive guests she brought to Bootle was Katherine Jex-Blake, the famous "Jix", a nationally respected authority on education and from 1916 to 1922 Mistress of Girton College.

However, the most poignant Speech Night may well have been in 1931, the first to be held following the tragic death from a brain tumour in 1930 of her brother, Frederick, a Minister in the Church in 1913 in Scotland. During WWI he had been appointed as a Chaplain in the RAF, and had taken up this role again in 1929. Tragically, in less than two years he had died, leaving a wife and a daughter. The following November, Ethel invited Group Captain McHardy, a colleague of her brother as Chaplain in the Air Force, to speak to the girls and heard Frederick described as "one of the best people he had ever met".

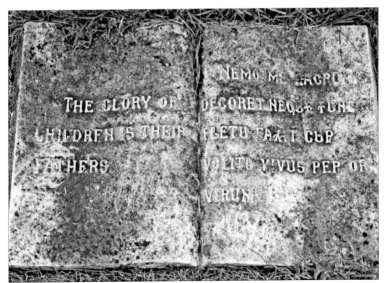

This was to be a hard time for Ethel, or "Queenie", as she was affectionately known within her family. In May 1932, just over a month since the opening of the new school on the Breeze Hill site, her father died aged 73. "Jack" Steuart was a personality in Bootle, and his passing attracted front page obituaries. It is possible to buy some of his books today on the internet. Among his most popular publications were a love romance of Robert Louis Stevenson, "The Cap of Youth" and one of Robert Burns, "The Immortal Lover"; he was particularly popular in the U.S.A. for his critical account, "Robert Louis Stevenson: Man and Writer".

Ethel herself wrote for publication too. Her best known work was "The Annals of Quintus Ennius" – still available on the internet. She also contributed on a regular basis to academic journals such as the *Classical Quarterly* and the *Classical Review*. Her classical background can be seen in the inscriptions on the grave of her father (and later mother) in Bootle Cemetery: one from the Bible and the other from Quintus Ennius.

Dr. Steuart and pupils

As Head Mistress of the BSSG, Ethel's first task was to lift the school after the death of Lydia Taylor who had been in the post since 1910 and had been a strong and very popular leader. Another was to play her part in moving to suitable accommodation for a growing and successful institution. The Breeze Hill site had been identified and earmarked already and, within six years, the move had been accomplished; however, as we have seen, this coincided with a period of personal sadness for her. She and her mother found a new home at 15 University Road, just off Merton Road. They lived here together with Minnie until Annie Maude's death in December 1945, only a short time after they all returned from evacuation duty in Herefordshire.

Ethel's next tasks now in 1945 were twofold: get the school back running smoothly following the years of war and evacuation and to oversee the transition to a Grammar School. The curriculum, however, changed little and the school was very similar to the one that had faced up to war in 1939. Ethel knew that she would retire as Head when she reached the age of 65; in March 1953 her successor was announced. Alderman Hugh Baird, Chairman of the Education Committee, thanked her for her "unflagging and distinguished service throughout 27 difficult years."

Ethel gave her final annual report to pupils and parents at the Speech Day prize-giving ceremony in the school hall on 28th November 1952. As always, the Hall was divided into two main columns facing the stage, decorated with flowers and the main party of Head and guests sitting at a table on the stage. The girls sat in their uniforms in rows of ten, with the senior girls sitting in the balcony at the rear of the hall. Parents occupied the other half of the hall and teachers stood or sat at the side and at the rear. Ex-pupils have told me how impressively Ethel appeared on these public occasions, dressed in her bright red gown: they were quite clear that while other staff wore black gowns with individually-coloured furs to identify their respective universities, their Head had worn a red gown. This was her scarlet doctoral robe from Cambridge University, completed by a wide, flat doctoral bonnet.

Dr. Steuart's main theme on the evening was to discourage the girls from taking part-time jobs as it would exclude them from weekend sporting activities and being a grammar school girl was itself a full-time job. "Girls who have worked hard at school all week – and their day is a long one – should get plenty of fresh air at the weekends," she said. The main guest speaker that night, Alderman Dr.L.Harris, thanked Ethel for her service and said that it was with great sorrow that he had learned of her retirement. "Those of us who had known her for many years, as I have, recognised the high standard she had given to the school."

Ethel remained in University Road until 1955 when she moved with Minnie to a village on the outskirts of Edinburgh, where she died in March 1960, virtually fifteen years to the day since she had returned to the school hall at Breeze Hill following the end of evacuation. She was 72.

Today, her ex-pupils still remember her very well as a formidable Head Mistress. As one of them said recently, "We were very proud of her."

CHAPTER 2 – 1930-1939

A New Building and Early Days at Breeze Hill

The school was established in its new, state-of-the-art building for 1932. There still remained the Preparatory Department for children aged 5 to 11. It was considered to be a great achievement for Bootle to have such an attractive school on a site that virtually overlooked the rest of the borough. However, in 1939 war was declared and resulted in evacuation from Bootle for the majority of pupils. The school was closed temporarily, but some pupils did carry on at Breeze Hill. Others joined the Boys' Secondary School in Southport. Dr. Steuart and many of her teaching staff ran an alternative school in a small town in Herefordshire called Kington.

The School Magazine for summer 1930 said, "*On May 21st the School attended the ceremony of the laying of the Foundation Stone at the new site in Breeze Hill. All are looking forward to removing to their new quarters in September 1931.*" The ceremony was reported in the *Bootle Times*, and we can find the Foundation Stone next to the front door of the Hillside building. The Stone was laid by Alderman Simon Mahon, JP, Mayor of Bootle at 3pm on 21st May 1930.

The ceremony was presided over by the Chair of Governors, Walter Scott, also the chairman of the Higher Education Committee for Bootle. He said, "We have experienced many obstacles not the least of which was the oft-repeated need for rigid economy. We had a similar scheme a few years ago, but it was turned down because of economy. We overcame those difficulties, however, and set about building what will be a great educational asset to Bootle. It is symbolic that the school has been placed on the highest spot in the Borough. The pupils of the school will look back with pleasure to the day when this monument to light and learning was built and the stone well and truly laid."

Walter Scott reminded those present that some years before, Bootle Council had been able to purchase the 10 acres of land on this site for a "small sum". "The occupiers of the houses that stood here were well-known to most of you. They have passed on to make way for the scholars... I hope that succeeding generations will realise how difficult it has been for us to carry on with this project. We have been faced with the censors who demanded public economy, but if we are to economise, education is the last thing we should touch. It is no good having a model town with an uneducated mob in the centre. Health and knowledge are paramount services to any centre."

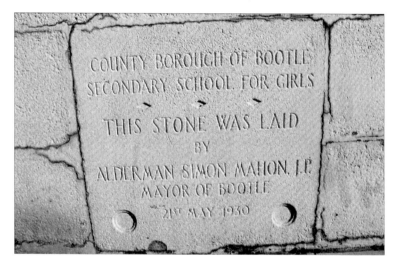

The Foundation Stone that can be seen outside the front door of Hillside

The Mayor, Simon Mahon, said, "We in Bootle feel that our children are as good as any in the land...I am an advocate of free secondary education. I know that some who are here may not agree with me but I believe that a secondary education should be given to every child capable of profiting by it, without cost to that child's parents...Many of us *have not had the opportunity of a secondary education, but we are trying to get that advantage for you.*" He asked the Governors for a half day holiday for the girls, and this was granted to great cheers from the girls of the school who were present at the ceremony that afternoon!

They presented what the *Bootle Times* called a "leaden casket" which would be buried in a cavity under the foundation stone and ready to be opened at some future time – what we call today a "time capsule". Into it they placed the names of everyone associated with the opening of the school as well as copies of the *Bootle Times*, *London Times*, *Daily Herald*, the programme of the day, the school prospectus and some coins.

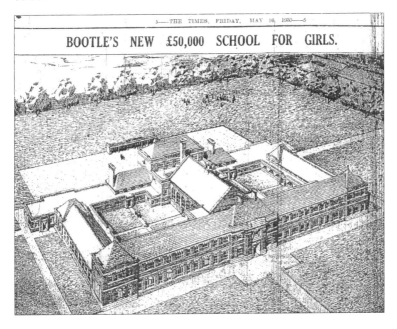

An impression of the new school prior to construction from a report in the Bootle Times in 1930

The cost of building was £50,000 with furniture and furnishings extra. The designer was Major Gilbert Fraser. The school buildings themselves were situated in the centre of the site for two reasons:

- to keep the school well clear of the sound of road traffic; and

- to centralise the approaches to the school building from all parts of the grounds.

Times change, of course, and some years later Bootle Council saw the need to widen the road on Breeze Hill from two single-lane carriageways to two three-lane carriageways, facilitating the greater need for access to the docks at one end and the Queen's Drive ring road at the other. This required the school to lose some of its grounds at the front, with the wall and gates and railings being taken and re-sited nearer to the school itself. At the same time access via the front drive was closed and all traffic was required to move via the Stuart Road entrance. A wooden board saying, "Beware of Motor Cars" remained on the school premises for many years after. The two side-drives were both accessible from the road and were also considered "cartways", telling us something of the nature of road transport at the time. A Lodge for the caretaker was planned but not constructed immediately – old girls remember that area being used occasionally for "nature study". The surrounding grounds were intended to be used as playing fields: 3 football pitches, 2 hockey pitches, 8 tennis courts and 2 basketball courts. Ex-pupils remember there being tennis courts on the site of the current Sports Hall.

The main entrance was placed centrally facing Breeze Hill with a direct approach to the Assembly Hall. This area of the school could thus be used independently of the remainder of the school buildings. It was used for both the formal ceremonies, in 1930 and 1932. The Headmistress's office was placed close to the front door, with a waiting room and office in close proximity. The Assembly Hall was designed to allow quick and easy exits. It was said that it had space for 660 people on the ground floor, with 160 more in a Gallery to the rear, though in these health and safety conscious days it does seem to be an awful lot of people! There was a stage at the front of the Hall – the same situation as the present day – and a changing room to either side. There was also a Projection Room on the first floor to enable films to be shown onto a screen at the front of the hall. BSSG was the first school in the country to have this facility. In 1932 the Hall was situated on the ground floor and all entrances/exits were on that level. It was only in the 1980s that the present-day Library was created and the Hall became a one-floor area entered from the second floor. The classrooms were placed along the corridors, though there were fewer than exist in the present day. They were placed to the east, south and west so as to ensure the full benefits of the sunshine during the school hours of the day. In 1932 there was no access to modern technology such as interactive whiteboards, televisions or even slide projectors!

The building provided two internal courtyards or quadrangles. The inside corridors were constructed to eight feet wide and were aimed at allowing free cross-ventilation to each of the classrooms. Cloakrooms were placed near the Southport Road entrance to the school: as in all secondary schools in the modern era, these have now been replaced for other purposes. Changing rooms were placed in the same area to provide easy access to the playing fields. In 1932 the Gym was situated on the first floor, with access on the same floor to more changing rooms and toilets. The original Gym is now used as two Art rooms. The outside Gym was built in the 1960s and the Sports Hall in 2006. Along from the changing rooms on the back corridor of the building were the Dining Room, Kitchen and Laundry, as well as Cooking and Housecraft rooms. The Dining Room provided seating accommodation for 140 pupils. In 1932 only pupils who lived further than a stipulated distance from the school were allowed to stay for a school meal; everyone else had to return home to eat. Lunchtime was from 12.15 to 2.00pm. Other rooms included the Art room, the Library (situated in what is now an ICT room), a staff common room and prefects office (both situated in the current Food Technology theory room). There was also a Medical Room in the Learning Mentor's office opposite the Dining Room. There were 2 Science laboratories on the first floor for Chemistry, Physics and Botany, with accommodation for 80 pupils in each! There was also a Lecture Room for practical demonstrations. Further, according to the *Bootle Times*, provision was made for a "gas service and drainage and fume chamber by means of false floor and flues: a science preparation room and dark room and balance room are in close touch."

1932

In 1932 the girls moved into their new school building. It must have been a very impressive building when it was first opened. Indeed, the teachers soon discovered that the polished parquet floors along the corridors proved extremely tempting for the girls to slide as far as they could. The teachers were soon placed on duty on the corridors at times of movement along the corridors! "No sliding, girls!"

The Opening Ceremony took place on the 8th of April, 1932, attended by the Earl of Derby and the Mayor of Bootle. The pupils lined the entrance to the school to welcome their visitors, the main entrance for cars at the time being from Breeze Hill itself. They then filed into the Hall for the first presentation.

This stone commemorating the opening of the school can also be found at the front of the building

BOOTLE'S £52,000 SCHOOL FOR GIRLS
"Temple of Light and Hearing" Opened By Lord Derby

Lord Derby with the Mayor and Mayoress and some of the chief guests, on the platform in the assembly hall, after his Lordship had performed the opening ceremony.

Can you spot the mistake in the sub-heading? It should say "Temple of Light and Learning".

SCHOOL ORGANISATION IN THE 1930s

Preparatory Department

The school still had a Preparatory Department for children under the age of 11 and who were working towards passing the 11 plus exam to gain entry to either the Girls' or the Boys' Secondary School; this lasted until 1946 when the school became a Grammar School for Girls aged 11–18. The "prep" classes were Forms C, B, A, I, and II. The youngest pupils at 6 years old were in Form C, and they then progressed until at age 10 they would be in Form II. In this year they were "prepared" for the entrance examination which they had to pass at the same standard as other candidates from other schools before gaining admission to the Main School. The age of transfer was at 11.

Main School

The work was planned as a five year course leading up to the "School Certificate". When girls arrived for their first year they went into one of two parallel forms, III A and III B.

They were taught in "sets" according to their ability in each subject for Maths, French and Latin.

They could then opt to stay on at school, so long as their teachers felt they could cope with the work. In these years they were prepared for the second examination – Higher School Certificate. Even after 1946, when the preparatory school and Forms C, B, A, I and II ceased to exist, the pupils in their first year at the Grammar School were called Form III.

The organisation and naming of form groups was more or less the same as when the school was opened in 1910.

> In Year 8 they were called IV and IVB
> In Year 9 they were called Upper IV
> In Year 10 they were called Lower VB and Lower VA
> In Year 11 they were called Upper VB and Upper VA

The Curriculum in the 1930s

- English
- Mathematics
- Geography
- History
- French
- Latin – and Greek for some years was an extra option for some girls in Form VI
- Science
- Drawing
- Domestic (including Needlework and Cookery)
- Singing
- Elocution
- Physical Exercise

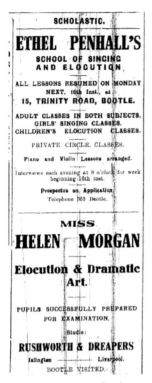

It is fascinating today to see "Elocution" on the timetable. All the girls in the A forms in the first three years had to take elocution lessons. It was delivered by a part-time teacher, Miss Helen Morgan, who gave private elocution classes in the area.

A music teacher, Ethel Penhall, was appointed at interview in 1929 from a shortlist of 5 candidates out of 32 applicants for the position of part-time teacher of music and singing at £50p.a. Singing and Music had become particularly important as, a short while earlier, a school inspection had recommended developments in this area.

Both of these teachers became particularly involved with stage productions at the school for years to come.

The pupils stayed almost always in their own form room for lessons with the teachers moving to them. They kept their pens, ink, ruler etc. in their desks, moving out only for Science, Art and PE/Games lessons. This continued to be the case for a considerable time, certainly well after becoming a Grammar School in the 1940s.

School Hours

Morning –   9.00 to 12.15
Afternoon – 2.00 to 3.15 (extended to 4.00 in 1940)

Many pupils did go home for their lunch, but not all were able to do so because BSSG took in girls from across the borough. The new school canteen provided meals for those who lived too far away. Those staying in school for lunch had to go outside into the Yard when they had eaten and wait there until the bell rang for afternoon registration and classes.

Mention has already been made about one pupil at school about this time, and who has still maintained links and visited Hillside a number of times. She is Jesse Besford, who was born in November 1918 – the month which saw the end of World War I – and she lived in 77 Garden Lane, Bootle, now demolished to make way for newer housing near the New Strand. She won a scholarship for BSSG and she was admitted on 12.9.1929. Jesse remembers very well being present at the ceremony to lay the Foundation Stone in 1930 as well as the official opening of the new building at Breeze Hill by the Earl of Derby in 1932. The girls lined up along either side of the front drive whilst the dignitaries arrived by car. She remembered her teachers generally with affection and said, "I had a good education, though I didn't realise it at the time." The teachers at school, always known as the "mistresses" by girls and staff alike, were almost always single women.

Miss Gwladys Williams taught English very well and had good discipline. "I thought she was a smashing teacher. She did have a sharp wit on her, though. I once asked her if I could lift up the lid of my desk. She replied that I could if I were strong enough. What I should have asked was "*may* I lift up the lid"!" She remembered Miss Mercer, later Senior Mistress, as being a very demanding maths teacher – "and I wasn't very good at maths!" Miss Morgan had a "well-rounded voice." Helen Morgan. as we have seen, worked at the school part-time as a teacher of "Voice Production" and elocution. She recalled the above-mentioned music teacher, Miss Ethel Penhall, who was a good singer: "she taught you theory in music and took it for granted that all of the pupils had a piano at home." In the 1920s, some homes certainly did have a piano, but the cost was certainly beyond the means of many people.

Jessie provided me with one of her school reports to her parents. She was thirteen years old and in Form Lower IV. Her teachers were as follows:

- English – Miss Williams, from Bangor, N.Wales, aged 50
- History – Miss Fairhurst, from Wigan, aged 30
- Geography – Miss Morrison, from Tadcaster, aged 54
- Algebra/Geometry – Miss Kerr from Liverpool, aged 28

- Latin – Miss Morley from Preston, aged 28
- French and Form Mistress – Miss Metcalfe from Manchester, aged 25
- General Science – Miss Benson, from Manchester, aged 42
- Drawing – Miss Bark, aged 61
- Needlework – Miss Barrow from Ambleside, aged 29
- Physical Exercises/Games – Miss McNaught from Waterloo, aged 28
- Elocution – Miss Morgan from Bootle, aged 40
- Music – Miss Penhall from Colwyn Bay, aged 49

					Report for the Year ending	
Name *Jessie Belford*				Age 13 Years 8 Months	Form L IV	
SUBJECTS	No exam ined	Result of Examination			REPORT ON YEAR'S WORK	
		Per-centage of Marks	Posi-tion	High-est Marks		
ENGLISH LITERATURE	27	57	7	67	Fairly good.	G.b.
ENGLISH LANGUAGE	27	74	2	76	Fairly good; examination result good.	G.b.
						G.b.
HISTORY	27	64	3	75	Good.	E.Th
GEOGRAPHY	27	51	4	79	Fairly good.	a.h.b
LATIN	27	74	5	87	Fairly good.	W.Ma
FRENCH	27	42½F	13	95	Fairly good.	J.S.
ARITHMETIC	27	62½	7	79	Fair. Could improve with	
ALGEBRA	27	42½F	13	95	a little greater effort	D.K.
GEOMETRY	27	31 F	11	67½		
TRIGONOMETRY						
CALCULUS						
BIOLOGY Practical						
BIOLOGY Theoretical						
CHEMISTRY Practical						
CHEMISTRY Theoretical						G
GENERAL SCIENCE	27	50	12	77	Fair.	H.H
DRAWING	27	51	19	76	Fair.	E.
NEEDLEWORK					Weak.	M.B
DOMESTIC SCIENCE						
PHYSICAL EXERCISES					Improving; must not	H.McN
GAMES					neglect remedial exercises	H.M
ELOCUTION					Fair.	E.P.
MUSIC Singing					Fair. Fair.	E.P.

Jesse also provided me with a copy of the School Magazine for summer 1930. It helps to give us a flavour of what life was like at the school as everyone waited to begin life in the new Breeze Hill building. Some of the highlights were:

- The Mayor's Ball at the Town Hall
- A Wireless Concert provided by prefects in the laboratory
- A visit to see the opera "The Barber of Seville"
- Visit to Crane Hall to see some plays in the French language
- Visits to Liverpool Museum and to Chester
- Speech Day at the Town Hall (the equivalent of our Presentation Evening)
- Helping Salisbury Road School with their Christmas party
- End-of-term Cake and Candy sale in aid of local charities
- A concert/play production entitled "Elizabeth Refuses"
- Helping the Mayor with appeals for donations for the Kiddie Kamp Fund
- Musical Society, run by Miss Penhall
- Presentation by Form V of "She Stoops to Conquer" at Christ Church Parish Hall, proceeds in aid of the Kiddie Kamp Fund
- Annual Gymnastic and Folk-Dancing Display
- Nursery Rhyme Fair in aid of the Helen Hunter Memorial Fund
- Ceremony for the Foundation Stone laying
- Sports Day
- Games – hockey, tennis and cricket

Jesse was working toward her examinations for the School Certificate when her father fell ill. Her family needed Jesse to leave school in order to get a job to supplement the reduced family income. They still hoped, however, that she could remain on roll to sit the forthcoming examinations. Unfortunately for her, her mother's request was refused and Jesse left without qualifications. Nevertheless, the fact that she had been educated at BSSG stood her in very good stead and she eventually found a good career for herself at Littlewoods Ltd.

CHAPTER 3 – 1939-1945

WWII and Evacuation

When war broke out in September 1939, it was not unexpected and much preparation had been made for possible attack on the UK by Germany. The nation had prepared for gas and bomb attacks. Evacuation was set up for all schools in Bootle, and over 6000 pupils from schools throughout the Borough were evacuated. In 1939-40 many BSSG pupils left Bootle for billets mainly in Southport, with Dr. Steuart and the teachers billeted themselves in Southport, Ainsdale and Formby. The Secondary School for Boys was evacuated to premises in Southport. However, there was little action at the start of the war for citizens of the UK, so little that it was called the "Phoney War". Children began to drift back home. However, things changed following the terrible "May Blitz" of Merseyside in 1941. After the May Blitz, there was a general consensus that children had to leave Merseyside for a safer environment.

All schools in Bootle were closed by the end of 1939 and a programme of evacuation begun. This involved all children and teachers, as well as roughly 7,000 under-5s and their mothers. They went mainly to Southport in the first instance, though there are many cases of children being sent into Cheshire, North Wales and parts of Lancashire. The 1946 school magazine looked back to the start of the war: *"Few who are now in school remember that hot Friday in September 1939 when we first went to Southport, and walked its streets until dusk with the harassed billeting officers. There, on the Sunday, we heard from the pulpits that war was declared, and many of us wondered if we should ever see Breeze Hill School again. Yet by the summer term all but a few of us had deserted our friends at St. Andrew's and were back in the old haunts, because the sky was still clear of enemy planes, and we all preferred home to the best billet."*

St. Andrew's Church was situated on Eastbank Street and remained open until 1968, after which it was demolished. One former pupil recounted how aged 14 she used to travel to Southport daily on the 14 bus rather than have to board there, and did so in the company of senior mistress Mary Mercer who also refused to be evacuated away from her family in Bootle. It took very little time, though, for children and parents to begin to return to Bootle.

Many parents did not want to send their children away, despite the potential dangers from bombs, and would not co-operate with the official programme. So many children returned home and were left unsupervised because their schools were closed that the Council applied to the Central Government to re-open the schools and bring the teachers back to run them. By January 1940 schools were open again, and it was not until the end of the school summer holiday that the first bombs fell on Bootle. "Then one dinner hour we heard our first siren," continued the 1946 Magazine. "That sound heralded three terms spent largely in the corridor air-raid shelters where at first we sang in nervous excitement, and later struggled with boredom and education under difficulties. The war came nearer and nearer to us.... Although there was another evacuation, most of us still plodded up Breeze Hill daily, and slept in shelters at night, and noticed more and more piles of debris where once there had been buildings." There were intermittent attacks throughout the autumn and winter. The bombing caused many of the girls at school to be up all night, often in public shelters or in makeshift home shelters such as under reinforced tables or in pantries or spaces under staircases. At Breeze Hill a selection of mattresses were placed in the Gym at the back of the building to give some girls the opportunity to catch up on their sleep. The teachers held practice sessions for the girls in responding to air raid warnings and putting on their gas masks in the corridors. They did this in earnest when the air raid sirens actually did sound. Girls could be caught out when returning to school from dinner, and would occasionally have to use an air raid shelter in Derby Park. In October, the Secondary School for Boys in Balliol Road was hit by two bombs, destroying the Pembroke Road wing. This school was hit twice more, and its School Captain Harry Swinton died whilst taking cover during a raid in a public shelter that took a direct hit. The building at Breeze Hill escaped damage, though some bombs had dropped within the school grounds and playing fields. There was also loss of life among the girls: Dr. Steuart talked of "Little Margaret Mumford, of the Lower Fourth, who perished in an air raid in 1940 – the only casualty the school suffered." BSSG welcomed a detachment of the Air Training Corps (ATC) to use its premises at Breeze Hill for drill and other training purposes in 1940. In 1943 the school also began to take in some of the newer admissions from the Boys' school due to the shortage of classrooms in Balliol Road because of bomb damage. The old Bedford Road School was opened as a storage space for the furniture of people whose houses had been bombed.

However, it was the May Blitz (2nd – 9th May 1941) that prompted rapid responses. It was probably the heaviest bombing attack on an English target up to that time: nobody living in Bootle then ever forgot its horrors. Nearly three-quarters of houses were either damaged or destroyed, with over 1,000 people being injured or killed and over 20,000 made homeless. Whole streets were obliterated and it was dangerous walking down roads and streets because of the craters in the roads as well as fires still burning. The photograph on the previous page from Sefton Libraries shows a house at 23 Breeze Hill struck by a bomb.

People who remember the Blitz have told us that the town had to go without mains water, electricity and gas supplies. Evacuees were now sent much further afield with destinations in Cheshire, Herefordshire, Radnorshire, Shropshire, Haydock and Wigan as well as Southport. Although the last bombs to drop on Bootle fell on 20th October 1941, the horrors of the May Blitz were so great that the principle of evacuation had been firmly established. "When the May Blitz came," said the 1946 School Magazine, "our numbers fell rapidly. On the Friday only forty girls (out of 600) attended; the seniors asked permission to go out to help with the emergency canteen work, and exhausted but undaunted fire fighters were glad to be invited to school to eat what would have been the school dinner. And how dirty we all were! Those were the days when even the water supply failed in some parts of the town." One of the teachers at Breeze Hill resigned her position and left the school on the 6th of May that year. This was probably a result of the bombing and example of the fear and desperation felt by people living in Bootle during the Blitz and, as such, the story of the school helps us understand the wider history of community and country. The Council acted swiftly and between the 9th and 15th May 851 children were sent to Shropshire, Radnorshire, Breconshire and Herefordshire. By the end of the month the number of evacuees had risen to 1,896.

The Secondary Schools for Girls and Boys worked together with Bootle Council to re-organise themselves to meet the needs of wartime and evacuation. The numbers given for pupils and teachers were those at the start of the scheme and were in a state of constant flux during the war period.

- Southport – premises in Marshside and St.Andrew's Hall in Southport became a "dual school" – today it would be called a "mixed" school - with 291 pupils (233 boys and 58 girls), led by Mr.Berbiers and a staff of 13 men and 4 women.

- Bootle – Breeze Hill became another dual school with 79 boys and 215 girls run by Miss Mercer as Acting Head with a team of 3 male and 6 women teachers.

- Herefordshire – Dr. Steuart led a party to the town of Kington and the villages in the surrounding countryside in Herefordshire to continue the education of the girls, using initially the premises of the local Grammar School for lessons on three days a week.

It was for the parents of each child to decide where they should be: evacuation to either Southport or Herefordshire, or stay at home and attend Breeze Hill.

At Breeze Hill, Miss Mercer and her staff had quite a job on their hands – none of them had any experience of teaching boys and it proved to be a challenge. Mary Mercer was born in Liverpool in 1884 and at the age of 57 she became an acting Head Mistress in wartime. The school attempted to carry on its work as much as possible. In December 1941, with so many of the normal school either in Kington or Southport, they held an end-of-term carol service. The *Bootle Times* reported that, "Hymns were beautifully rendered by a choir of boys and girls, and solos were sung by pupils from infants to seniors. Harmony, too, was delightfully executed by the choir who had been very well trained by Miss Ethel Penhall, who accompanied at the piano."

At first it was difficult to place the pupils into recognisable forms for teaching and, with the increasing number of attendees, the space available for teaching lessons became an issue. Mary Mercer later recalled once opening the door of a classroom and announcing to the mistress in charge of the class that she would have to take another pupil. The mistress replied, "If you bring any more, will you please ask the Education Committee to put bunks round the walls?" Gwladys Williams also recalled her experiences of working at Breeze Hill at the time. At her Retirement Presentation in 1942 she said, "I should like to say how glad I am that the boys and girls in school last year have shared in this presentation. I consider that last year was a very special one, because it marked the first dual school in Bootle. It was difficult for masters and mistresses as we had to change our methods. Some pupils who came to school had no intention of doing any work: *"the staff were determined that they were here to work, and so the tussle began. I am not at all sure who won! But as time went on the difficulties lessened and unity grew. Before the end of the year all were happy. Some were working very well, and others more than they had ever worked before! The prefects helped very considerably, and I hope that the present prefects are helping to the same extent.... I must not forget the old boys whom I have taught – or, at least, tried to!"* Gwladys Williams had formally retired in the previous summer, but returned to Breeze Hill for a term due to a constantly changing teaching staff. The co-educational challenge began to work successfully and the pupils enjoyed play readings and debates together to share and appreciate other people's points of view, games, concerts and clubs. Anyone who could knit – many in those days – spent hours producing items for the armed forces. In all, the pupils and teachers together developed a real sense of comradeship throughout their time of war.

HERGEST CROFT, KINGTON AND HEREFORDSHIRE

The small town of Kington in Herefordshire was the site of the evacuation for a large portion of the pupils at BSSG. Their adventure began at Ford Station in Bootle, each pupil carrying a label with their name and address. They travelled by train down to Hereford before changing trains and arriving at a station near to Kington by tea time. They were met by a number of local people who had agreed with billeting officers to take in evacuated children from the school. The pupils themselves, however, after a long journey to a strange rural place and having left their families earlier that day, found it a very uncomfortable experience, especially as a number of local people had been expecting younger children and were unwilling to place an older girl in their homes. Matters did improve, however, as the girls woke up the next morning to find a warm welcome in most cases and were astonished at the entirely rural area to which they had moved. Some had other children there to play with, but many of them found themselves a long way out of the central town of the evacuation, Kington. For the first two weeks or so they were left to settle into their new surroundings and begin to write letters home to parents in Bootle. They quickly learned about rural life and, for some, life on a farm. They found themselves often out in the open air and "going brown"; they went fruit picking, and earning money for doing so; they joined in haymaking and apple-picking. If they went hop-picking they would be out at 7.45 a.m. and return home by about 6.30 p.m., earning roughly one pound and four pence each a week.

The Lady Hawkins Grammar School, Kington

The teachers were in billets with local families, mainly in Kington though Dr. Steuart stayed with her mother Annie Maud and her maid, Minnie, at the Burton House Hotel in the centre of the town.

In the first months of evacuation, the girls were taught at the Lady Hawkins Grammar School, sharing the premises with the 84 Kington scholars; the BSSG girls used it on Tuesdays, Thursdays and Saturdays.

On Sundays they would all troop along to the local Church opposite the school for the service. Pupils billeted outside the town were brought in and returned home by bus, it being quite common for the bus to pick up a pupil at about 9 a.m. and return her home by 6 p.m. One of the interesting aspects of this sharing of premises by Bootle girls and Kington boys and girls was that it enabled them to make contact with each other and send messages via letters left in the schoolroom desks! Through the means of the letter drops in the desks, the girls and boys got to know each other well. They would often write to each other and then meet up somewhere, though this was not formally permitted by the teachers who kept a really close eye on them. The Bootle teachers appeared to be quite strict with the girls. Lessons and learning were still very important, even during wartime, and the aim of the older children was to pass the School Certificate at that time. Not all pupils were entered for this– there would be a class of between 15 and 25 pupils possibly, each paying three "guineas" (three pounds and three shillings, or £3.15) a term.

Hergest Croft as it is today

Meanwhile, the Bootle Education Committee agreed with the Ministry of Health on the lease of a large house in Kington called Hergest Croft, which had been requisitioned by the Government for use in supporting school evacuation. Hergest Croft is always pronounced "Har-guest" and not "Her-guest"! It was, and still is, owned by the Banks family who were at that time living elsewhere. Today, Hergest Croft is open to visitors to walk through their beautiful gardens and grounds and is certainly worth a visit. It lies along the Offa's Dyke walking trail and at the edge of Hergest Ridge. A few minutes' walk up the road will take you to the remains of an old house called Hergest Court. This has a remarkable link with the famous Sherlock Holmes story of "The Hound of the Baskervilles". The story was set by author Sir Arthur Conan-Doyle in Bovey-Tracey and Grimpound on Dartmoor, but was inspired by the legend of Thomas "Black" Vaughan and his "Black Hound of Hergest". The name Baskerville derives from a powerful Norman family who lived very near to Kington at Eardisley Castle and later at Clyro in which town can be found the "Baskerville Arms". Conan-Doyle himself is said to have stayed near Kington at Dunfield House whilst editing the final version of his most famous novel.

Hergest Croft had been built in the final years of the 19th century and contained a large number of rooms suitable for use as accommodation and for teaching purposes. It was to be used mainly for the School Certificate pupils and most of the girls had to remain in their local billets. Only 36 girls, together with an adult complement of 12, moved in. Towards the end of the war, another house in Kington, "The Close", was taken over for a brief period for use by more Bootle girls.

In April 1942 there was a service of dedication at the Croft, modelled on the service held at Breeze Hill in 1932 for the opening of the new school building. Dr. Steuart had composed a hymn for that event and this was sung again. The *Kington Times* reported that "*the Head Mistress is Dr. Steuart and in an interview with our representative she made the interesting statement that the BSSG is the only school in Bootle undamaged. As is well-known, Merseyside suffered a terrible series of 'blitzes' and Bootle had its share.*" Alderman Jones, the Chair of School Governors, said "*... they had had to seek the aid of good souls in many places and finally they made contact in Kington with a bunch of Good*

Samaritans ... he had never met anything in all of his travels to equal the beauty of Hergest Croft with its extensive and well laid-out grounds." The Director of Education for Bootle, Warwick Bolam, described how many Bootle people had lost their homes temporarily, their children and their possessions, but they had not lost their indomitable spirit, and he said to the girls: *"You are not going to let down your parents."* That same spirit was there in the younger generation and he was sure they would enjoy their stay in the country and would return after the war better and wiser, broader minded and more tolerant as a result of the inter-mingling of the country with the town.

Sybil Shepherd and Pat Hughes were given the opportunity to move from their billets to Hergest Croft because they both had elder sisters, Barbara Shepherd and Joan Hughes, who were in the cohort of girls needing to prepare for the School Certificate examinations. These were the girls in Upper V, Lower VI and Upper VI. In fact, although the two girls had been happy in their billets, there was also good reason to be pleased about going to the Croft, or "The Hostel" as they generally called it. As they were both billeted in the countryside they were not really near any other Bootle girls. Also, there was quite a long walk each morning to meet the bus. On the way home, the bus would not leave the Croft until 5.20 p.m. and, even if it was on time, would take about thirty to forty minutes to get home. On Saturdays they were in school all day and were tired when they arrived home, ready for their tea and their washing-up duties before being in bed by about 7.30 p.m. There would be more spare time and less travelling for the girls at the Croft. Lessons were given in a large room at the rear of the house that had previously been a dining-room. On Saturday 14th March 1942, the pupils began the move into Hergest Croft to live, and by the next week all had arrived: despite regular changes of pupils and teaching staff, it remained their own virtual boarding school for the remaining three years of the war.

The photograph taken that day with Bootle's Director of Education, Warwick Bolam, shows all 77 of the evacuated girls in Kington at the time. The girls put on an exhibition of singing and dancing, enjoyed a party and the girls in billets went home at 7.30 p.m.

To look after the girls there was a team of teachers and other staff. Dr. Steuart had a small suite for her use with her mother, Annie Maude, and her family maid, Minnie. The Housekeeper/Matron was Mrs. Poole, the Cook was Mrs. Crease and there was a housemaid called Elizabeth. For illnesses the girls would visit a local doctor and, in those pre-NHS days, pay for the service. There were usually four teachers staying at the Croft, and amongst the earliest were the following, for each of whom I have shown where they came from and their age in 1942.

- Muriel Smalley, 34, was from Lancaster and taught English. She was a kind, well-organised and popular teacher who continued her career at Breeze Hill until retirement.

- Annie Morley, 38, was from Preston and taught Maths. In December 1946 she left Breeze Hill to become Head of Roberts School in Bootle. She was thoroughly well-organised and popular. Girls remembered her wearing "the most beautiful skirts, especially some particularly nice Italian knitted skirts".

- Jennie Kneen, 30, was from Waterloo and taught Geography.

- Mary Carter, 24, was from Farnham, Surrey, and taught art and crafts. She was very popular with the girls who felt she brought a touch of glamour to the Croft. Whilst she was at Kington she also organised the hockey, rounders and tennis teams, as well as look for opportunities to take groups of girls on walks and visits outside the town. At a time of shortages, she was an art teacher with little access to painting materials, so she placed greater emphasis on architecture and was keen to use examples from the Herefordshire area.

- Sadie Sadler was an art teacher from the North-East of England who arrived after Miss Carter left. She made a good impression on the girls, and gave them her copy of *And Quiet Flows the Don* to read in their dormitory. At this time, giving pupils a copy of a Russian novel was quite daring.

- Miss L.E. Ims taught History and was new to BSSG when she arrived at Hergest Croft in February 1942. She was very well appreciated as a teacher; however, she was quite old-fashioned in her ways. As one former pupil said, "We're talking real school ma'am days, but she was a fabulous history teacher." It was noticed that she spoke more informally than the mistresses did generally. One girl wrote home that she had fainted on the way to class and was taken there by two other pupils. Her teacher was Miss Ims, who took the girl in then said to a prefect in the room, pointing to the small seating area just outside the classroom, "Get the kid on a chair and chuck 'em both outside." The girl commented, "Miss Ims uses terrible slang!" How times have changed.

- Kathleen Watson, 44, from Bootle – she was in Kington only for the summer of 1941, and by the autumn she had returned to Breeze Hill to resume her role as Senior Mistress in the Preparatory Department at Breeze Hill. Kathleen Watson is a name associated with Hillside High today as it is her name that is given to one of the awards at the modern day Presentation Evening.

There was a continual fluctuation in the teaching staff throughout the years of evacuation. However, two of the stalwarts who are still remembered by former pupils today were Miss Morley and Miss Smalley. At the end of the war, Miss Morley went on to be Headmistress of Roberts Primary School in Bootle whilst Miss Smalley remained on the staff of BSSG after the war and eventually became Senior Mistress until her retirement. One former pupil who attended the school after the war described Miss Smalley as her best teacher "who never raised her voice but had a demeanour which demanded respect". They were popularly known by the girls as 'Mo and Smo'.

It was not until the 30th of March 1945 that pupils from both Kington and Southport returned home and were welcomed back to the school at Breeze Hill by the Mayor and the Head. This was the last party of Bootle children to return to the town. The girls evacuated to Southport had returned home earlier in the same day. Even before their return, entrance examinations for the Bootle Secondary Schools were announced in March 1945 in the *Bootle Times*. They were new exams that replaced the previous "Special Place" exams. Candidates were to be aged 11-12 on the 1st of August with special consideration for children of 12-13 years who were unable to take the previous year's examination or who were specially recommended by their Head Teachers as late developers.

This photo taken during a picnic at Hergest Croft in 1943 shows three teachers: Annie Morley, Muriel Smalley and Sadie Sadler

CHAPTER 4 – 1945-1972

The Post-War Years and the Grammar School for Girls

These were years in which the school returned to normal, or as normal as life could be after such a momentous event as the Second World War. A number of teachers took the opportunity to retire. Life at Breeze Hill returned to one as a Secondary School for Girls and, very soon, Bootle Grammar School for Girls.

At the end of the war in 1945 the school gradually returned to how it had been in 1939. Once again it was a secondary school for girls. The 1944 Education Act created three different types of secondary school: grammar schools, secondary technical schools and secondary modern schools. The three types of school would all be for pupils aged 11-16/18 and were intended to meet different needs with the most academically-able children attending a grammar school. However, there was no smooth changeover in Bootle due to people's different opinions on whether children should be put into these different types of school. Some argued for something similar to the present comprehensive schools and no 11 plus exam to get into a grammar school. Prior to the 1944 Act, the "secondary school" was the equivalent of the grammar school and prepared pupils for the School Certificates. However, the system of naming schools had now changed and Bootle moved from having two "secondary schools" to nine of them, the others having previously been "elementary" schools or "central" schools. There would be no grammar school. This led to a fierce debate within the Education Committee and a public debate carried out within the pages of the *Bootle Times*. Eventually, the "battle of the schools" was settled at a meeting of the Education Committee to call the two original secondary schools "grammar" schools. The debate had taken eighteen months to resolve from when the ruling Labour group of the time decided not to differentiate between the old secondary schools and the new ones. "*It is recognised that the work done at (the original secondary schools) ... is the same work as is done at all grammar schools,*" said J.A. Merrick when he moved the motion to adopt the name of grammar school.

Whilst there had been a change of name to "Bootle Grammar School for Girls" (BGSG), little had actually changed other than the removal of the preparatory department. From 1947 onwards, entrance to the school was through an 11 plus exam sat at the local Primary School. Pupils found that they may still have been using old stock notebooks and exercise books, but new stationary with "Bootle Grammar School for Girls" printed on them were beginning to come into general use. The building always impressed the new entrants, particularly the large traditional school Hall with the interlocking wooden seats (that were still in use well into the Hillside years) and the balcony at the rear of the Hall. The pupils would sit facing an impressive stage set out with a wooden lectern (also used for many years for Hillside assemblies) and seats usually for three people. At morning assembly this would be the Headmistress, the Deputy Headmistress and the Head Girl. Above the stage was a plaster coat-of-arms of Bootle, designed to be in perfect perspective for those sitting in the Hall and looking up at it. Today it has been preserved and re-sited in the main entrance hall to the school. Those with keen eyes will be able to detect the slight difference in perspective when looking at it straight-on.

Assembly was held every morning with teachers present, standing down the sides of the hall. The music teacher would play on piano and the girls would sing hymns. At some time in the early years of the Headship of Dr. Steuart the school adopted a song to be its "school song".

Written in 1924 by Martin Shaw (Lyrics) and M. A. MacDonald (Music), "Brave Hearts Adventuring" was also known as the "Girl Guides Song": at the time of writing this song, Martin Shaw was the Chief Commissioner of the Girl Guides Association. It was also used by many other schools, and former pupils from the 1930s onwards remember it well. It was sung poignantly at the memorial service for Gwladys Williams in the school hall in 1942 following the singing of her two favourite hymns.

> *Glad hearts adventuring, the way is wide,*
> *Valour and faith shall shield the pilgrim's side.*
> *Constant and undismayed, your journey past,*
> *Across the hills of time, home lies at last.*

> *CHORUS*
> *Glad hearts adventuring, the city of God dawns –*
> *Take to the trail again, sisters follow the star.*
> *Honour and sleepless love, where're ye roam,*
> *Shall watch beside the camp and guard the home.*

At Friday assemblies the girls always sang the hymn, "God be in my head and understanding" by Jared Anderson. The Head, Senior Mistress and Head Girl would sit on the stage; the Senior Mistress would read out notices and prefects would give readings. Former pupils can remember all the girls being spoken to very firmly by the Head Girl on occasion. On the wall was a board listing pupils who had gone on to university.

The floor was beautiful parquet, as was to be found throughout the rest of the building including the corridors. Indeed, as previously mentioned, it had been realised by teachers and cleaners very soon after the opening of the school in 1932 that these polished wooden surfaces made an ideal skating rink for the pupils! Jessie Besford remembered that when she joined the school in its first full intake in 1932, teachers would line the corridors to prevent the illegal skating activities that we saw had appeared when the girls first moved in. School rules prohibited running along the corridors. Those girls found transgressing the rules would fall foul of the school behaviour system. As can be imagined, bad behaviour was not something that was a real problem in either BGSG or BGGS. This can be imagined quite easily from the pressures faced by teachers transferring from BGSG to Hillside comprehensive in 1972. The system in the 1950s, and which had been in use since the late 1920s, was known as "signatures": if caught doing something against the rules, the pupils had to go to Dr. Steuart's office to write down what she had done in the "Signatures Book". On their Report at the end of the year it would be shown the number of times she had been reported. However, teachers did have to endure cheekiness and leg-pulling to whatever extent their teacher would allow it. Some teachers did terrify their pupils, whilst others had a much lesser effect. One teacher was unable to pronounce the letter "R", particularly unfortunate as the middle letters of her name were "RR"! She would often tell girls to "put your bewwy on your head", whilst it took little time in the school for girls to catch on to taking their rulers and running them along the ribbed radiators at the side of the classroom so that this teacher would say, *"Don't wattle your wulers along the wadiator!"* So many former pupils remember that!

At Speech Day in November 1950, Dr. Steuart told her audience that this would be, *"the last time we shall see examination certificates appear as School Certificate. Next year we will have the General Certificate of Education which will involve changes of age limit and standards of attainment, but I must add a word of warning... It stands to reason that there will be more people holding the new certificates, so that the quality of the certificate will be more important than ever."* The numbers of girls attending the school at this time were high. All pupils were expected to attend Speech Day with their parents on the appointed Friday in November; however, the number of pupils being so buoyant, the building was unable to accommodate all seven years at once. Therefore, one year ("the third forms") had to have their own celebration evening early in the New Year.

Dr. Steuart and the staff, with the school cat which seems to have adopted the school and was fed from the school kitchens

Prizes were awarded for pupils from each form throughout the school. It is lovely to see a link between past and present through the "special awards" presented each year; indeed, these awards were published in the *Bootle Times* a couple of weeks prior to the Speech Day, giving us an insight into the honour they bestowed and the prestige of the school within the Bootle community. The special awards in 1950 were as follows:

H.A.Hunter Memorial Prize (in memory of the Senior Mistress 1910-1929): Vivienne Perkin

Gwladys Williams Memorial Prize for High Character (in memory of the highly respected teacher of English 1907-1942): Juanita Woods (photograph shown below)

Kathleen Watson Memorial Prizes for English at School Certificate (in memory of the teacher and former pupil who had died suddenly in 1947): Vivienne Perkin, Margaret Carr, Beryl Moran, Kathleen Franklin, Sarah Lamont

Sir Benjamin Johnson Scholarship (Sir Ben was the founder of Johnson's the Cleaners and a leading figure in Bootle education in the early years of the 20th century): Margaret M. Clarke and Joyce M. Marshall

Lydia Taylor Scholarship (named after the first Headmistress 1910-1926): Mima Hesketh, Norma Kelly

Special Prize for Empire Knowledge: Doreen Roper

Whilst the prize for "Empire Knowledge" is a throwback to a lost era, the Williams and Watson prizes are still awarded today.

Balliol Girls School put on a production of William Shakespeare's *A Midsummer Night's Dream* at the end of the summer term in 1950.

6——THE TIMES, FRIDAY, JULY 14, 1950——6

A MIDSUMMER NIGHT'S DREAM

" A Midsummer Night's Dream" has become so much an entertainment for the Christmas season that it is now very difficult to imagine it as it must originally have been produced. It is the fashion in the professional theatre to introduce a full corps-de-ballet of fairies in muslin, a gibbous moon, devised by the electrician, vast settings, and music by Mendelssohn. Why this should be, when Shakespeare's word-music can create a much more wonderful "Wood near Athens" than any stage carpenter, must be solved by wiser heads than ours. At any rate, when the pupils of Balliol Modern Secondary School performed the play last week, they went right back to the Shakespearian style. They draped a green ground-cloth over a couple of forms, and left the rest to the imagination of the audience and the actors.

Purists might raise the objection that schoolchildren with an appreciation of Shakespeare's verse, and the ability to put the verse across, are rare birds indeed. Shakespeare is all too often drummed into the heads of children in such an unimaginative manner that the strength of his craftsmanship eludes them, and they leave school determined to have as little to do with his work as possible.

Again, to many children Shakespearian English might almost seem like a foreign language—almost like acting Molière in the original French! All difficulties taken into account, the Balliol cast gave a better-than-average rendering of this elusive play. Their successes were decisive, and, though they failed at times, they may reflect that " The Dream " is rarely completely successful on the professional stage.

Bully Bottom is a part which lends itself to a boisterous, unsubtle style of playing. His self-conceit as the leading actor in Peter Quince's cry of players, his ass-headed love for Titania, his awakening, and the foolery of the Wall Scene, give great scope to the actor, and Sylvia Jenkinson made of the part a likeable country bumpkin, with expressive face and expansive gesture. The role of Peter Quince the harrassed producer, gave Gloria Inglis the chance to prove herself the least self-conscious of the performers, and the other Athenian mechanicals, Flute (Beryl Lucas), Snout (Vera Atherton) and Snug (Isobel Johnson) provided some bright moments.

Dorothy Jordon lent Puck an expressive, "fey" little face, and an elf-like manner. There was little rhyme or reason in her airy, dancing movements, but her obvious enjoyment of the part communicated itself to the audience.

The lovers have the most thankless parts in the play, and though Doris Rimmer (Lysander), Beryl Davenport (Demetrius), Catherine Bullen (Hermia) and Joan Carew (Helena) did their best, one was unimpressed, and couldn't have cared less whether their romantic tangle was sorted out or not.

Others in the cast were Violet Sheridan, Judith Gill, Myra Knill, Dorothy Yates Georgina Yool, Maud Blutes, Ethel Jones, Rachel Wise, Shirley Tasker, Gyllian Eyes, Sandra Jones, Audrey Wheatley, Sheila Malley, and Lena Robinson.

Mrs. Louisa, Miss Mills and Miss Hughes were responsible for production Miss Pickering and Mrs. Roberts for costumes, Mrs. Clark for scenery, and Miss Owen for the background music and effects.

Uniform was still worn. One change, however, was in the headwear. Before WWII the girls' headwear had been a velour hat. In the 1950s this changed to a navy-blue beret. The full uniform can be seen in the photographs, with a summer uniform with white blouse available for months with warmer weather. In the 1950s there were still "coupons" for virtually everything – or so it seemed at the time – and finding the correct uniform was always a problem for families. The girls had to wear blouses made of "tussore", a strong coarse brownish Indian silk and with a dark ivory/creamy colour.

Gym slips had to have wide pleats. At the time, the Gym was situated in what eventually became in 1972 the Art Rooms – look carefully and you can still find the evidence. In the 1960s the school acquired a purpose-built gym and, eventually, a sports hall. In the photograph of girls having a gym lesson (in the present-day art room!), it is surprising to see the pupils wearing their school ties! As it happens, this gives a false impression. Former pupils have said that this was done solely for the taking of the photograph and that normally PE lessons were taken in open-necked shirts and knickers! They did, of course, have access to plenty of space for outside activities such as hockey, tennis, rounders and netball. In the 1950s they had a good reputation for hockey, though the days of fielding a cricket team as in the 1920s had long gone.

In April 1953 the junior hockey team, for example, won the Liverpool and District Frank Sugg Challenge Cup, the first time that the trophy had gone to Bootle. The winning team comprised the captain, Joan Hynes, School Games Captain Dorothy Howard, Sylvia Jones, Patricia Thornton, Marjorie Knight, Joan Dowick, Pauline Cotton, Sylvia Tritton, Maureen Stinson, Joan Crolley, Christina Smith and Jean Slater.

Despite the change to a new school system, the naming of Years and Forms was retained. Therefore, girls began their first year – the present-day Year 7 – as Year III. This was split into three groups, A, B and C. Based on the 11 plus examination results, the teachers would have decided already which girls were most likely to be successful in the School Certificate and in their second year at the school would find themselves in set A. Those in set C would be identified as less likely to achieve academic success and would have a timetable containing less of the Classics and more of Cookery and practical subjects. With a school leaving age of 15 prior to 1973 many of the girls in C and even B would leave before their final year.

The old Library – now an ICT room

The curriculum had changed only little since the opening of the building in 1932. It consisted of English Language and Literature, History, Geography, French, Latin, Biology, Physics, Chemistry, PE and Scripture. The aim at the end of five years was to pass the School Certificate initially and, later, the GCE examinations. For the "School Cert.", a pupil needed to pass an examination in a minimum of five subjects, e.g. English Language supplemented by four other subjects such as Literature, French, Maths, Geography, Latin, History, Science. It was a simple "pass" or "fail" with the results published in the summer in the *Bootle Times*.

Two science rooms

A classroom for English

Miss Smalley, Dr. Steuart and Prefects

The school said that, "Considerable use is made of the prefect system. In particular each form below the VI has one prefect particularly attached to it, to give such help as she can to both Form Mistress and girls."

There appear to have been few extra-curricular activities other than for the successful sporting girls, but the grassed areas, fields and tennis courts around the building were greatly appreciated.

For a large part of the 1950s the music teacher was Mr. Stewart. He can be seen in the photograph of the choir practice in the hall, opposite, and is fortunate enough to have help in playing the piano from pupils.

We can see pupils in the back row standing precariously on stools and a pupil playing the piano. There continued to be a tradition of music and singing at the school and there was an annual school production. On page 66 we see the happy cast of *Alice in Wonderland* in 1954/55.

Dr. Steuart's final address at a Speech Day was in November 1952, though she was guest of honour the following year. A photograph printed in the *Bootle Times* shows the old school hall as it was with the stage party facing the rows of girls in uniform on the right-hand side and on the balcony, the parents on the left and teachers standing at the sides and back.

The School Play in 1954-55 – Alice in Wonderland

On Speech Days, the hall was laid out formally, the stage bedecked with flowers and a platform party of between ten and a dozen. This would include an invited guest speaker, the Mayor and Mayoress, the Chairman of Governors, the Town Clerk and the Director of Education. They would sit on comfortable chairs on the stage, with the prizes laid out on a table in the centre of the stage. Dr. Steuart spoke, as she always tended to on these occasions, to the parents rather than the girls themselves. She asked the parents to discourage the girls from taking part-time jobs at the weekend as being a grammar school girl was a full-time job, saying, "*Girls who have worked hard at school all week – and their day is a long one – should get plenty of fresh air at the weekends. I know at this time of the year it is a temptation to them to earn a little extra pocket money...*" If parents did this, she concluded, they would be doing their share to promote a brighter future for the country because a generation of healthy young men and women was even more important than increased production. The music, presented by the school senior and junior choirs and prepared by Mr. Stewart, included:

> "I waited for the Lord" – Mendelssohn
>
> "Anenomis" – George Rathbone
>
> "Brother, Come Dance with Me" – Engelbert Humperdinck (1854-1921)
>
> "Wake up" – Montague Phillips
>
> "The Countryman" – Peter Warlock
>
> "The Ride of the Witch" – Charles Wood

In July 1953 Dr. Steuart enjoyed an evening of reminiscences at the school with a group of old-girls and current members of the school. Edna Brown recalled "*the rising applause when she came to Speech Day after retiring.*" She was presented with a gold watch and bracelet, purchased through pupil and teacher subscription, by Director of Education.

In September 1953, Miss Dorothy Vivian Blyde took over as Head of the grammar School. She was the ex-pupil of BSSG who was Head Girl in 1921-22; her late father had been a well-known teacher in the borough, particularly Gray Street and Bedford Road Schools, who had retired having given fifty years service and was particularly noted for his musical activities. She had actually attended the funeral of Helen Hunter with her parents in 1929 and had spent eight years at the Balliol Road site. She went to university at Liverpool and Caen to read for a degree in French and began a career in teaching in Liverpool before moving to Shirebrook Grammar School for Girls in Derbyshire. She too had a strong interest in music and taught French and Music.

In her first address at Speech Day in November 1953 she raised the importance of choosing the right job following time spent at the BGSG. "*In my short time here I have been able to realise that there should be much stronger sense of ambition among the girls...The choice in matters of character and career lies in your own hands,*" she said, speaking directly to the girls themselves. Miss Blyde presided over a school that changed little in curriculum or approaches to learning. One thing she did change was the school song, replacing "*Glad Hearts Adventuring*" with "*Jerusalem*". One pupil commented, "*I think she had waited since being a pupil to do that ... I did not approve!*"

'Choose Jobs Wisely,' Says New Headmistress

A PLEA for girls to show more ambition and originality in choosing jobs, was made by the headmistress of Bootle Grammar School for Girls (Miss D. V. Blyde, M.A.) at the school's annual Speech Day last Friday.

Presenting her first annual report since her appointment, Miss Blyde said she would like to see more girls staying on until the Sixth Form. It would be better if the girls chose a greater variety of jobs than at present was the case.

"The parents should ask themselves," she said, "whether they are encouraging their daughters to make the best possible use of opportunities in their grasp. In my short time here I have been able to realise that there should be a much stronger sense of ambition among the girls. I appeal to parents to play their part in supporting the school's endeavours."

The Power of Choice

Addressing her remarks to pupils and old girls, Miss Blyde said she would like the girls to learn the meaning of the word discrimination. This was the power of choice. It was the real meaning of education. To be able to use the power, they needed to have knowledge. They could not choose wisely in ignorance. "The choice in matters of character and career," she said, "lies in your own hands. Think carefully before you choose."

Earlier, Miss Blyde had said that although it was less than three months since she had taken up her appointment she had already had an [...]

Guests and girls at Bootle Grammar School's Speech Day listen intently as the new headmistress, Miss D Blyde, M.A., appeals to girls to choose their occupations wisely.

D.V. Blyde remained in post for 14 years, retiring in July 1968. As she retired, Bootle was on the verge of making all its secondary schools into comprehensive schools: at a celebration in the main hall she said, "*I think loss of the grammar school is very saddening, not only in Bootle but throughout the country. Comprehensive education has its place but, in this age we are striving too often for uniformity, either in people or in things. Examinations are a necessary feature of education.*" She believed that with the new system there would be bound to be a lowering of standards.

The First Year class in summer dresses

Five years later – in the Fifth Year

The school before the widening of Breeze Hill

On her retirement, the post of headmistress of BGSG was taken by Mrs. J.P. Whitely until the school was finally closed in order to amalgamate with Balliol Secondary Modern School and become Hillside High School in 1972. The move towards comprehensive education was a national strategy and each LEA had to develop its own solution. The first comprehensive school, catering for 1,050 pupils aged 11-16 across the ability range, would be opened at Breeze Hill in September 1969 through extensions to the Grammar School building; the pupils would come mainly from BGSG and the two Balliol Secondary Schools. The costs would come from funds raised a few years earlier to provide a new building for the two Balliol Road schools, but Council thought it better to build one large new school on one site to create a comprehensive school and prepare for the raising of the school leaving age (ROSLA) from 15 years to 16. Pupils wishing to continue their education at VIth Form would do so at the mixed VIth Form College in Netherton.

The plans for the extension building originally included a school swimming baths on site, but this was never built. The two Balliol Road schools were merged into one but there was no "school on one site". When Hillside finally emerged as a comprehensive school it was in 1972 and was part of Bootle's whole LEA plan for new High Schools across the borough. Not only that, it was opened on two sites and utilised both schools' existing buildings. Hillside was not to be a one-site school until quite some time later.

CHAPTER 5 – 1972-2012

HILLSIDE HIGH SCHOOL

The story of the modern school that is Hillside today began four years before the school itself was opened in 1972. In February 1968 there had been a formal announcement that Balliol Secondary School for Boys and Balliol Secondary School for Girls would merge into the new Balliol Secondary School for the following September. They were longstanding schools with their own history and traditions, and there was no little concern among parents and teachers in both as to what lay ahead. The Headmaster of the School for Boys, Stuart Elliott, became Head of the newly amalgamated school with the Head of the School for Girls, Miss M.S. "Stella" Evans, becoming Deputy Head. Even at this distance of time it is clear that this would have been a difficult time for teachers at both the Balliol schools as well as those of the Grammar School for Girls, as this was only the first step towards a full amalgamation into a new comprehensive 11-16 school due to take place shortly, with September 1970 the expected target date. That needed to be postponed to 1972, the date by which the whole of the Bootle LEA was to change wholesale to a comprehensive system.

There were positive reports in the *Bootle Times* about activities at the Girls Secondary School despite the impending changes. This included a school trip to Mons and Brussels as part of the Bootle-Mons twinning programme and a celebration for Miss Evans at the school on its final day of 28 July, 1968. It was widely accepted that she possessed a very sharp eye and missed nothing that was happening in her school. Despite this, her colleagues managed to organise a whole school assembly at the end of the day for pupils and parents to say, "Thank you, Miss Evans." She was asked by her Deputy, May Watts, to go along to the assembly hall where she found every member of staff and all pupils awaiting her together with the well-known "Auntie Margaret" of the *Bootle Times Herald*. "Overcome with emotion," reported the *Bootle Times*, "Miss Evans thanked everyone for the wonderful surprise. When she had received a bouquet at the prize giving that morning she had naturally thought that was the end and these presentations had quite overwhelmed her. She pointed out that they had come to the end of an era, and when the school reassembled in September they would be joining with the boys, and she hoped that they would set a good example." The new Balliol Secondary Modern School existed from September 1968 until September 1972, the full list of new High Schools in Bootle being published formally in November 1971 and a programme of staffing structures and appointments taking place over the following two terms.

The New School

The name of "Hillside" was chosen as something that represented the site of the school but was new and not associated with any single one of the previous schools. It was clear to Bootle Education Committee that a two-site school was unsatisfactory and that at some time in the future a decision would have to be made to teach all the pupils at just the one site at Breeze Hill. In 1972, however, there were too many pupils to accommodate on just one site and not enough money to adapt the Breeze Hill building at a time when funds were very much in demand for work on the whole range of newly amalgamated and adapted schools in Bootle. Work was done to adapt the old Balliol Road buildings for the needs of the day. In particular, a number of workshops were created in an open plan style at the heart of the old building. Open plan, however, was not to the taste of the teachers using that area and slowly but surely temporary structures were put into place so that by the end of the first year of the new school they were enclosed classrooms to all intents and purposes. Another innovation that was not to the taste of many of the teachers was the move in both sites to mixed staff toilets. One cause célèbre was the feeling stirred up by one of the male teachers who would cycle to school and then park his bicycle just inside the entrance to the mixed toilet outside the Quarry Road staffroom: this caused quite a storm among the staff! Within a few years, single sex toilets were restored to the staff. Toilets for pupils were always single sex.

Money also had to be spent on adaptations to the existing Breeze Hill site for the opening of a mixed school for the first time since the years of World War II: toilets for the boys became an imperative, with the old cloakrooms quickly becoming redundant and new changing rooms for the area close to the newer 1960s Gym provided. Technology rooms for woodwork, metalwork and technical drawing were set up and, in order to provide sufficient space for the teaching of art and design, the old BSSG gym was taken over and remodelled into two art classrooms with a teachers' store area. The remodelling work was carried out by the new Head of Art, Gordon McColl. Gordon never rushed anything: he simply assessed what needed to be done and then got on with the job. The work he undertook in 1972 has endured for many years now. The wall bars and other facets of a gym were clearly to be seen when he started and, even today, it is not difficult to recognise its original purpose.

The 1960s gym and the school fields would now be the heart of PE and Games at the school, though there was some hope at the time that a new Sports Centre for Bootle would be constructed at the end of the Stuart Road playing fields nearest to the school so that pupil access to it would be very easy and thereby provide the Hillside children with excellent sporting facilities on their doorstep. This was not to be, however, and following much discussion within the Council it was decided to build the new sports centre just off Maguire Avenue on the grounds of the old Bootle Stadium. Hillside paid for pupils to use Bootle Sports Centre for many years after that, but at the cost of many difficulties for teachers ensuring they arrived and departed on time. It was a significant problem for PE teachers as well as for the person writing the timetable. Eventually, the problem of not having a purpose-built sports hall for the children simply became too great. In the early years of the 21st century, Hillside made applications for funding to build a sports hall and plans were drawn up. With the proposed building costing so much money, it was a political as well as an educational issue; fortunately, Hillside did have friends within the LEA who supported a final application and Hillside was given the green light for a brand new sports hall. This success was not without its pain for the PE teachers and the pupils who had to withdraw from using the facilities at Bootle Stadium to ensure the school's case for having a sports hall was strong enough to succeed. That meant delivering classes in an unsuitable yard environment for over a year, but eventually it served its purpose and ever since the children of Hillside have enjoyed the top class facilities that they always deserved.

The first Head Teacher of Hillside High School, David Terry BA, MA (Oxon), born in 1935, was a mathematician who had worked in two grammar schools and one comprehensive school prior to arriving in Bootle. He had been appointed two terms before the opening of Hillside so as to give him two terms to develop the structures of the new school. With office premises in Bootle Town Hall, he conducted an exhaustive series of interviews to appoint the staff, comprising many teachers from the amalgamated schools as well as from other schools within Bootle and from outside the area. In September 1972 there were 990 pupils with 55 full time and 4 part time teachers: 9 teachers had come from the BGSG, 17 from Balliol and the rest were new to the school. Within the first term, 7 teachers resigned or left the school.

Some of David Terry's major challenges included the organisation of a school on two sites, managing the amalgamation of pupils from a very mixed educational experience, managing the amalgamation of teachers from two existing schools, implementing his philosophies of education and school life on teachers, pupils and parents and establishing a model that would meet the needs of all the children. This was, clearly, to be no easy task. It involved many grammar school teachers dealing with boys and mixed sex classes for the first time. By the time that Hillside returned in September 1973 for its second year, most of them had left.

The new school management system included people from the existing schools: Stuart Elliott was made Associate Head (though he was to retire at the end of the first year);Stella Evans became Deputy Head with responsibility for the Breeze Hill Site; the two existing Balliol Road Deputy Heads became Senior Teachers; and a team of three new managers from outside Bootle were appointed to significant and influential roles as senior curriculum leaders. Mrs. Whitely of the Grammar School did not take a role at Hillside. Many teachers from the existing schools accepted jobs; where there was an area not sufficiently covered or a new post was created, people were brought in from Bootle and beyond. The whole of the new staff were brought together on the Breeze Hill site for a first staff meeting in the summer term of 1972.

In that first year there were many challenges to face for both pupils and teachers, and it took a long time for the school to settle down as a mixed comprehensive school. It was always going to be difficult to bed down an amalgamation of two very different institutions into a system of organisation and teaching that virtually none of the teachers had encountered previously. On top of that it was a school based on two sites with all the problems that brought, and then the ideas of the new Head were markedly different from what had gone before either in the Balliol schools or BGGS. There was to be no school uniform from the first day and corporal punishment was banned. They were both major issues at the time. In terms of uniform, most schools in Europe manage very comfortably without any uniform. There is a different perception in the UK, and many parents and teachers felt that the standards of the old schools had been reduced at a stroke. Moreover, the fashions of the early 1970s were quite outrageous anyway and pupils (and some teachers) would attend school with bell-bottom trousers, high heeled boots and shoulder-length hair. Clothes were often highly-coloured and flowing, a development from the flower power years of the late 1960s. It was to be at least two years before school uniform returned following an open vote by parents and teachers.

It is easy for us to forget today that in 1972 and for a number of years after, Hillside was a school on two sites, Breeze Hill and Quarry Road. The original aim was simply to create one new school on the Breeze Hill site, but with over 800 pupils needing places that was not possible. Split sites always cause some problems or other, no matter what is used as a solution. The new Headteacher, David Terry, was faced with a need to merge the two schools into one and develop its own identity and ethos; he also had to deliver the promise made by Bootle Council to the parents of the girls at the grammar school to provide their children with a "grammar school education". In order to create a feel of one school and not have an "upper" or "lower" school, Terry decided upon a system of Years 1, 3 and 5 (7, 9 and 11) on the Breeze Hill site with teachers moving as needed and occasional movement between sites of pupils to use specialist facilities or the playing fields at Breeze Hill. David Terry explained his ideas on grouping children for teaching and pastoral purposes to the staff in a circular prior to the opening of the school and dated 25.4.1972. He wrote: "*The three main objections to grouping children by academic ability are that to do so is (a) socially divisive, (b) inaccurate and (c) difficult to alter, owing to the self-fulfilling consequences of categorising children.*" He was fully aware of the challenges that a comprehensive model gave the school and recognised that "no one in the school would feel competent to undertake completely heterogeneous teaching groups to all ages. This and the fact that the older children have been following different curricula, compels some form of streaming, banding or setting for at any rate the older children in Hillside."

In terms of a general pastoral organisation, he intended to have a horizontal house system with Years 2 and 4 at Balliol and Years 1, 3 and 5 at Breeze Hill. His reasons were that it was the best numerical fit into the existing buildings, it allowed more of the senior staff to be concentrated at one site, teachers would easily be able to teach different age levels and it would better promote a sense of responsibility with the older pupils. The children in Year 1, the first fully comprehensive year, were initially placed into two parallel mixed ability groups with three forms in each group. Later, they were re-allocated into three ability bands. The new Head described his vision of education as "*more than the transmission of knowledge and values, more than the intellectual and emotional development of each individual.*" In a statement to staff in August 1972 he wrote, "*As children grow older we must try to increase the area in which they are able to decide for themselves. But one cannot act responsibly in an area of freedom unless one has a sense of justified self-confidence. To increase the self-confidence of each child must be a prime aim of any school. We do this by encouraging each child to develop his own qualities as far as he is capable, not in order to triumph over his contemporaries but to enable him to contribute distinctively and valuably to the well-being of others.... Concern for the individual will predominate in all we do as teachers."*

There was built into the timetable of teachers a "crossing rota" by which a teacher crossing sites would meet and escort a group of pupils crossing one way or the other. This entailed crossing two busy dual carriageways and was, of course, an unpopular duty for teachers who had to escort the pupils across the road. It did prove for a number of years to be a significant nuisance for pupils and teachers. When teacher timetables were drawn up, not only were the teachers who had to cross the road to deliver lessons on the other site required to escort a group of pupils, but also teachers who had a non-teaching period following the morning or afternoon break might be required to help with the "crossing duty". The same thing applied when groups of pupils were walked down to the Baths for swimming lessons.

The behaviour management programme was a cause of much debate. Hillside High School at the time of writing in 2012 is an object lesson in the successful care and development of children to help them through their education and present them with a vision for their future. That does not mean that the school does not face any issues and challenges from children, but there is such a strong child-centred ethos at Hillside backed up with a determination that children will succeed that all but the most intractable problems are solved by the end of Year 11. In 1972 behaviour of pupils was a major issue and there were very different opinions about what worked best among the staff. A team of five "Year Tutors" was created to monitor the pastoral welfare of the children, one each responsible for a year of pupils.

The different experiences of the teachers in terms of pupil misbehaviour were quite wide and some who had only experience of the Grammar School found certain classes extremely challenging. Many teachers, though by no means all, felt that the use of the cane was necessary to maintain good behaviour throughout Hillside. In fact, the use of the cane did return to Hillside in the mid-1970s until the Government banned corporal punishment in state schools in 1986. The Hillside of the 1970s and of 2012 are thoroughly different institutions, but the children come from the same area and the climate of behaviour in the modern-day school that has no corporal punishment is at a completely different level than it had been in the days of the 1970s and 1980s. This is not to diminish the efforts of the teachers at the school in the early years of the comprehensive school – the manner in which the school had been set up, albeit with the best of intentions, had given everyone very little chance of success. It was to take many years before a commitment to developing the curriculum and approaches to teaching and learning as a whole school replaced the continual search for a workable behaviour policy. It took years of progress and a thoroughgoing commitment to a child-centred approach for the school to gradually become the outstanding institution that it has become today.

The experiences of the pupils in their first year or two were also very interesting. The Education Committee had promised the parents of the girls of the Grammar School that they would all enjoy a "Grammar School education" whilst they were at Hillside. They were maintained in their own form groups – beginning in the second Year as the first Year was fully comprehensive from the start - and were taught in these groups; there was a good deal of dissatisfaction, however, among many parents who felt that the quality of the education they received was not good enough and that the climate of behaviour in the school was an inhibiting factor. External examination results were very disappointing. Many years later, some parents felt they had been deceived and let down by the politicians in terms of the "grammar school" promise. The girls themselves found some difficulty in adapting to new systems and a mixed school containing boys.

In terms of uniform, David Terry was aware of the difficulty facing parents from two different schools with existing uniforms in having to start fresh. He wrote to parents in July 1972: "*The uniform of either of the existing schools is perfectly acceptable, but please do not replace a uniform with a similar one when it wears out. At the moment we do not have a badge or a tie. I hope these will be available by the end of the first term. In the meantime, if you wish to dress your children so as to identify them with the school then boys should wear a black blazer with dark trousers and a blue or blue-patterned shirt. Girls should wear a navy-blue skirt, pinafore dress or suit. Blouses should be blue or blue-patterned and cardigans, pullovers and jackets should be navy blue. Any parent is free to send a child to school dressed differently provided the child's attire is suited to the circumstances of school life. Parents may not send their children to school in heavy footwear or jeans. And whatever is worn must, of course, be clean and tidy."* Whatever he intended short or long term escaped the notice of the children: to them this simply meant *No Uniform*! That, in the early 1970s, meant that anything went. It would be a couple of years before uniform made a return, voted back by parents and teachers. In his report to Governors later the same term, the Head wrote that, *"... there is no compulsory school uniform. My fundamental objection to this is that I do not see that I have the right, even if supported by a majority of parents, to seek to compel any particular parents to dress their child in clothes of someone else's choosing, providing what their child wears is clean, tidy and does not get in the way when performing any of the tasks of the school."*

The amalgamation of the schools and the introduction of a comprehensive school model were always going to be major challenges for the Education Committee and the staff on the ground at Hillside. Even at the time, however, and without the benefit of hindsight, it was clear that the opening of the new school was unsatisfactory despite all the tremendously hard work put in by everyone. The pupils were keen to be involved and there was a great deal of camaraderie amongst them, and the commitment of the staff was clear to be seen. They wanted this to work, but unfortunately there were too many differences in opinion of how the school should be developed. The changes that were introduced by the new Head were forward-looking and had real merit, probably the right direction in which to move to develop a comprehensive school. However, it was done all at once without a suitable period of preparation of the teachers: as such, the staff in general was not at ease with the Head and uncomfortable with changes that they felt undermined their ability to do their job to the best of their ability. They felt challenged by much pupil behaviour. Within two years, David Terry had left the school, leaving for a Headship at the Headlands School in Wiltshire in 1974. His philosophies of education had not been embedded in the school.

Pupils at Presentation Evening in 1976

The new Headteacher was Donald Duckworth, previously the Deputy Head of a school in Bolton. Stella Evans was acting Head for a term before Mr. Duckworth was appointed to begin in January 1974 by the Local Education Authority (LEA) with an eye on providing stability through a more traditional routine to school life. He remained as Head until 1990.

A retirement celebration for Senior Master Ken Argent (centre), previously of Balliol Boys' School. Making the presentation is Don Duckworth and on the right of the photo are Stuart Elliott and Stella Evans.

In Don Duckworth's time there were some important changes made to Hillside. Probably the most significant was the remodelling of the Breeze Hill building to provide a "one site school". In March 1986 the school saw the end of a two-year and £1.5 million programme of refurbishment; and in September of that year all of the 2nd and 3rd year pupils moved over to Breeze Hill to join the rest of the school for the first time. Previously, Don Duckworth had changed the organisation of the school so that Quarry Road became the base for the Lower School and Breeze Hill that of the Upper School. This provided a more compact structure and cut down dramatically on the movement of pupils as well as of the staff. The work had caused considerable inconvenience to pupils and teachers alike during those two years with corridors suddenly being blocked off with walls and classrooms being unavailable. The result was imaginative and very successful, though there was a knock-on effect of reducing the number of pupils at the school. The new school was intended for about 500 pupils, the size envisaged decades earlier by the LEA: the school never settled for long at that number, however, and was always considered to be a building that lacked sufficient space for the numbers of children it attracted. The modernisation came about following considerable criticism and pressure from school governors, the parents' association, parents and teachers. By 1984, they believed, the school building had become a pale shadow of the structure opened to children in 1932. Don Duckworth suggested that Breeze Hill was in a poor state and Quarry Road was far worse – *"something that Dickens was well familiar with"*: he was quite right. The architects made a real effort to blend the new elements in with the existing style and structure, right down to retaining the same type of stone and brick for the new-build classrooms. The major changes to the building were:

- 12 new classrooms added to the side and rear of the building's second floor;

- the sub-division of the Assembly Hall into a new Library on the ground floor and a drama hall on the second floor;

- the decoration and re-equipment of classrooms throughout the school, and the use of suspended ceilings;

- modernisation of the cafeteria area with new school kitchens;

- new changing rooms with showers for pupils taking PE and Games lessons;

- new offices for Year Heads as well as some extra storage areas;

- new toilets for pupils at either end of the building; and

- improvements in the heating system which was switched over to gas, though this has not been seen as successful throughout the years, particularly with reference to the heating of the Drama Hall.

The change to the Assembly Hall was particularly striking: the old stage area went, as did the balcony at the rear of the Hall. The ground floor area of the Hall was reduced so as to provide a Careers office and reception centre opening onto the existing Foyer. This change provoked much discussion at the time but it was an imaginative and bold move. In a reshuffle of rooms, the old Library upstairs became the staff room – it is now an ICT classroom with associated offices.

We have mentioned some of the prizes associated with people awarded at the annual Presentation Evening. Three prizes have been created since the 1980s to remember two pupils of Hillside who died tragically during that decade plus another in the first decade of the 21st century. In August 1982, 16-year-old Tim Stephens was selling newspapers with some other friends at the traffic lights of the Mons crossroads. Tim had completed his exams in June and was awaiting the results to take him on to his next step in education. Indeed, Tim was an exceptionally able boy who found academic work stimulating and engaging whilst having such a strong and imaginative personality that he threw himself into all sorts of extra-curricular activities. Only a little while earlier he had played the lead role in the school production, "The Toytown Terror", in which he saved Toytown "when Noddy went bad". Tim's results were excellent and he would have had the world before him, except that in walking over to a car to sell a newspaper he walked into the path of a lorry and was killed. Tim had two brothers, Jonathan and Simon, both lovely lads themselves; his parents were the Reverend Richard and Sylvia Stephens. Richard Stephens was the vicar of St. Matthew's Church in Bootle and was a strong friend of the work done at Hillside, on one Presentation Evening delivering one of the most inspirational and supportive presentations ever given.

Lee Nicol was a lovely, polite and well-mannered boy who loved his football. He lived in the Knowsley Road area of Bootle and had been a model pupil since beginning at Hillside. It was his terrible misfortune at the age of 14 to be in the Leppings Road end of the Hillsborough Stadium for the FA Cup semi-final against Nottingham Forest on the 15th of April, 1989.

Luke Eccleston was a quiet but extremely popular pupil who enjoyed taking part in as many activities in the life of the school as possible. He was a founder member of the school Eco Club. He died suddenly and quite unexpectedly of an acute heart condition during a Summer School activity in on 30th July 2009, just 2 days after his 14th birthday. As he was a great fan of C.F. Barcelona, his sister and a group of his school friends celebrated his life by going to Barcelona to visit the Camp Nou stadium and paying their respects with a short time of silence there. Following his death, the school established an Eco Award which is presented annually in his memory.

I remember all three of these wonderful lads well and it is so terribly sad that they lost their chances of happy and fulfilling lives at such young ages: in 2012 Tim would have been 46, Lee would have been 37 and Luke would have been 17. There were other young Hillside pupils who left us far too early, before they had ever had their chance at building a life. They include Rachel McGowan, who left in summer 2004 and died a few weeks later in a car accident; and Phillip Callaway, who died of a brain tumour in 2006 whilst in Year 9. We have tried to keep the memory of these young people alive in school in a garden landscaped with a pond and specially selected trees and shrubs. It is called the "Memorial Garden" and is a beautiful oasis of quiet reflection.

One of the most persistently happy memories for many ex-Hillside pupils involved the first two weeks of the summer holiday each year. During that time, groups of pupils enjoyed two separate weeks of "School Camp" at Satterthwaite in the Lake District. The Summer Camp had been inherited from Balliol Boys School. It was originally developed by woodwork teacher Bernie Wright, having negotiated a suitable venue in Satterthwaite in the Lake District with local farmer

Ewart Wilson. In the summer of 1972 the first of many Camps for the new school was led by Tom Wallis, Dave Mumberson, Dave Evans and a succession of teachers such as Pat Molloy, Bob Prescott and John and Lynne Neilly who were happy and willing to give up their own time to ensure the Camps ran well and the children had an unforgettable time.

However, there were still problems with pupil behaviour. In 1984, Don Duckworth spoke of the need to return to discipline, not just in schools but in society as a whole. At Presentation Evening he said, *"Those of you have gone through this school know we preach the philosophy that freedom brings with it responsibility. Everyone wants freedom but few are willing to accept the responsibilities that inevitably come along. The last decade's assumption that, at best, discipline is anti-social and that freedom is an ideal that elevates man to virtual perfection, can only be judged by what we experience and see."*

Throughout all those years, though, no one could question the commitment of the parents and friends who supported the school and the pupils through the offices of the Parents' Association. Hillside has always enjoyed unequivocal support from many committed parents. A photo from the *Bootle Times* shows the Head with retiring committee members Joan Fazakerley and Ben Roberts, among others; among the team can be seen Barbara Rouse, who has also served for so many

years as a School Governor along with present Chair of Governors, Hilary Raffell. Parents giving up so much of their time with their advice and support have always been an essential ingredient in the life, times and success of Hillside.

There were a number of different uniforms that were used at Hillside in the years since 1974, including one version without school blazers but instead employing a sweatshirt with a school motif. There were often problems in ensuring pupils wore their ties and school shoes.

In recent years, however, the current uniform with tie, shirt and black shoes has been maintained particularly well and Hillside pupils are recognised for their smartness. This has not happened by accident, and the high standards are expected from all pupils with any pupil reporting to school without their full uniform being required to work away from their usual form group until full uniform is restored. The results speak for themselves. Today, pupils wear white or blue shirts according to their Key Stage and each Year has a different coloured tie: prefects wear a different colour tie again.

There were plenty of other activities that brought recognition to Hillside in these years, including being one of only 6 schools in England to be invited to take part in the "European Studies – Ireland and Great Britain Project" which used history, geography and ICT to develop programmes of active learning and thereby provide Hillside with the opportunity of sending the first school-to-school e-mail on their new BBC computers. There were also regular Christmas and summer productions including the "Toytown Terror".

John Martin is a Merseyside-based comedian and after-dinner speaker who was a pupil at Hillside from 1974 to 1979. In the 1990s he approached the school, wanting to "put something back" for the current crop of pupils. With the particular help of Dick Carr, he began what was to be a series of 10 years of "talent shows" in which pupils vied one spring evening each year to win the trophy and a financial support in their chosen area. Ray Livingstone won the first award as a comedian, and later winners included singers, dancers and other young comedians. Eventually, with the school going from strength to strength in a range of different performance areas under the leadership of Carmel Carey-Shields and Nigel Richardson, the "Talent Competition" ceased to run and John used an alternative route to support his old school by raising funds for charity with comedy evenings at Bootle Cricket Club. It would not be fair to single out any names, but the whole school community is justly proud of the way in which performance has become a vibrant and exciting part of school life. Any pupil, starting from Year 7, has the opportunity to become involved and this has meant an enormous amount to so many of the pupils in the school.

Today, Hillside has the vision that creative expression is vital to the development of every child, and that expressive and performing arts enable pupils to develop social and technical skills. Pupils are encouraged to express themselves creatively to gain confidence and experience a real sense of achievement. Carmel and Nigel have taken artistic levels to new heights in terms of quality, imagination, verve and sheer range of performance. Creativity and involvement in drama, music and dance has become embedded in the life of the school of today.

In 1990 Don Duckworth retired and was replaced by his Deputy Head, Colette McDonald. Colette had arrived at the school five years previously and began to take on some key challenges, including the challenging behaviour of many pupils and the arrival of Ofsted and school league tables for examination performance. In her first act as Headteacher, Mrs. MacDonald called together on the first day of term all of her senior staff in the school library to ask the question: what are we going to do to make the pupils realise that this school belongs to them and that they should be fully involved here? She had been particularly successful in working with pupils who found traditional schoolwork very demanding and was determined to find ways to improve pupil performance as well as to make them feel that this was their school and that they were important. In her short term of office, having to retire through ill-health after 5 years, Mrs. McDonald placed her focus on the needs of the children and how the teachers should meet those needs. She was concerned particularly with pupil welfare, the best means of organising teaching groups so as to involve children of all abilities and to ensuring that pupils realised that this was their own school. It was during her tenure that Ofsted and school league tables first appeared and it was clear that many challenges lay ahead for the teaching staff. She retired and went to live happily in a beautiful spot of the Lake District, but she had left her mark. The challenges facing the school needed to be faced squarely and the Governors set about the task of finding a permanent replacement. After once false start, they tried again, this time with much better luck and enormously better judgement.

They appointed Mrs. Laetitia Shemilt, previously Deputy at Lowton High School in Leigh. Born in London, she was delighted to have been given the opportunity to work at Hillside and knew as soon as she visited the building that this was the place she wanted to be. What would be the direction the school would take? How would the school seek to meet the targets set for raising achievement? To the great good fortune of pupils and parents in the local community, the incoming head was uncompromisingly child-centred and fully committed to doing whatever needed to be done to help the pupils reach their potential in whichever field they wished. At that time, no one could have foreseen quite how successful the school would become over the next fifteen years or so, and it wasn't something that happened immediately. Change began slowly and it took some time of trying out ideas to find solutions that worked well. The key factor that held the changes together, however, was the commitment to child-centred education and the determination of the staff to make the changes work. There was a shared ethos that grew and developed until eventually the difference could be seen clearly in both the results in examinations that the pupils were beginning to achieve and the attitude and positive attitude that children were showing about the school. Of course the behaviour would never be perfect and there were always children who rejected school life and behaved badly with teachers and with other children, but where there were problems there was a team of pastoral staff growing in confidence and supporting each other to find the right solutions. There was always movement and development on the pastoral side to find the best solutions and to meet each new challenge posed by central governments, but with each change came greater expertise and a shared confidence and belief in what they were doing. The pastoral care and support given to children today is a mark of the quality of the school. In the days of BSSG and the Grammar School, these problems did not exist in the main. In the early years following amalgamation the work of the pastoral year tutors was amongst the most impressive in the school, though too often they and the teachers were forced into "fire fighting" problems. In the way that the amalgamation was carried out, the situation could have been little else; the present system has been allowed to grow organically and meet current needs appropriately, all within a well-defined ethos of caring for children.

For all the effort and good will put into the development of Hillside from 1972, it took some time for the school to really find its way forward and develop an ethos that would help the children of Bootle and Walton to have the confidence and the self-belief to produce results in external examinations that would lead to Hillside becoming recognised generally as an excellent school – rated "outstanding" by Ofsted, the Government's inspections body, in 2007. This also came to fruition eventually through a commitment by all the staff, whether they were teaching or support, that children lay at the heart of all that was done at the school and that Hillside was unequivocally "child-centred". By the time of the 80th anniversary of the opening of the new building at Breeze Hill, it was generally recognised that the approach of pupils towards visitors was exceptional and one extremely experienced educational adviser – an ex-head teacher himself – said that the behaviour of pupils at Hillside was the best in all the schools he visited across the North-West.

Many former pupils may have enjoyed their own time at Hillside in the past, but too many of them were critical of what they had experienced and were not all willing to send their own children to Breeze Hill. By the 1990s this impression had become outdated, yet needed to be confronted. In the early years of her headship, Laetitia Shemilt had a sign placed high on an outside wall for all to see: "Excellence in the heart of the community". This was a statement to everyone that the standards of the school were now very high and if you came to Hillside determined to succeed you would do so. There was no need to send a child to a school outside Bootle: you would not find better than Hillside now. Indeed, even children who did not want to work for their own success found that their teachers would not let them escape from meeting their obligations. Senior managers visited local primary schools to meet parents, but the clinching factor for a parent and child over choice of school was the annual Open Evening. Children entering the building could never fail to be impressed by the bright, welcoming atmosphere and the sheer amount of stunning, imaginative and colourful pupils' work displayed on the walls of both the corridors and classrooms throughout the school. Add to the mix the welcome given by the staff, and then add on the magic final ingredient: the pupils themselves, dressed smartly in school uniform and eager to show off what they were able to do in school. All volunteers, the pupils each year are the best ambassadors the school could have.

In 2008 Mrs. Shemilt was recognised for what she had achieved at Hillside when she became the North West of England Headteacher of the Year in a Secondary School. In being awarded this honour, she was described by the Awards committee as follows: "Laetitia Shemilt does nothing by halves. She is passionate about providing the very best education for all pupils, regardless of ability. Her ethos is that the education provided by Hillside High School must be good enough for her grandchildren – or it is not good enough for anyone else's! Her enthusiasm, passion and heartfelt belief that inclusive education is the key to improving the prospects of future generations are firmly embedded in the school's philosophy. Colleagues describe her as caring and kind, but with a 'backbone of steel' when needed." An ex-pupil of the Girls' Grammar School was moved to write: "*I was at Bootle Grammar School for Girls from 1964-69. I enjoyed it and did well enough, but so many didn't do well. Youngsters as bright as buttons fell by the wayside, lack of confidence made for diffidence – and I have always feared that it would remain the same... Thank you for enacting hope and giving deep value to the current generation of youngsters and for being a model of what is possible in Bootle."* Another letter of congratulation was sent by John Rolfe from the British Council in London, a man well aware of what Hillside had achieved over the years: *"Best wishes on your hugely deserved success! You make Hillside such a very special place for global teaching and learning – your support in ensuring that school has also received the DCSF International School Award three times is also tribute to your fantastic vision and complete professionalism...well done and a sincere thank you from the British Council."*

The Modern Hillside 2012

In 2009 Laetitia Shemilt defined the aims and special features of the modern Hillside. *"Our Mission Statement is 'Excellence in the Heart of the Community'. We believe that by working in fellowship with staff, pupils, families and neighbours all of our hopes and dreams can be jointly aspired to and achieved through excellence in teaching and learning, progress, academic standards, care and guidance and opportunities for all. In these ways we challenge our pupils to have the courage and self-belief to make their visions reality, enabling them to take their rightful place in society enriching it in so doing. We have an unwavering belief that our children can succeed. To facilitate this we have an ethos of high expectation and achievement which is totally child-centred, ensuring that pupils from all groups share this belief. We strive to make school a safe haven where talent and ability can be nurtured and developed. The emphasis is very much on the individual child and upon a pro-active approach which identifies and removes potential barriers to learning. Our teachers and support staff are highly committed and work together to achieve this by providing effective teaching and learning as well as care and support."*

Science Specialist Status was awarded to the school for Science in July 2004, when the school saw the need for a rigorous, academic subject to inspire and challenge its community to greater self belief: in particular, there were real concerns about the life opportunities for girls in modern society. An additional Science laboratory and a resource base were built and equipped. In March 2009 Hillside was designated a Specialist Languages College as well as achieving High Performing Schools Status. The school was also given a Gifted and Talented focus to allow it to drive standards in the pursuit of excellence and enable it to increase the number of pupils achieving top grades across the curriculum.

The behaviour of pupils at Hillside in lessons and around the school was judged outstanding by Ofsted in their most recent inspection of October 2007: it was reported that "students take a mature and responsible approach to their learning." In the letter to pupils, the Inspector wrote, "Your behaviour around the school and in classrooms is exemplary." Pupils have a Form Tutor who they see twice a day and who generally can be found throughout the day. There are Progress Managers and full-time Learning Mentors. Pupils are trained each year to become peer mediators and peer mentors, providing an additional layer of support for pupils who may prefer to talk to another pupil.

Appropriate to the success of the 2012 Olympic Games and the challenges raised for our modern society, a programme of Healthy Lifestyles has enjoyed a significant success at the school. The pupils reacted very positively to changes in the school dining hall and there is always an excellent take-up of a variety of foods which has allowed them to develop healthy eating habits. School meals are managed 'in house' by a trained and committed catering staff. Cold, filtered water is available free-of-charge in three locations accessible to pupils, with fresh fruit and bottled water 'subsidised' by the school. Sporting activities are, as ever, extremely popular with the additional facility of an excellent sports hall. PE is an integral part of the curriculum. Football, netball, cricket, athletic and basketball teams are entered in local after school leagues and perform well. The Sports Centre, opened in 2006, is a superb facility and includes a large sports hall, two classrooms, a multi-gym, facilities for disabled users and reception area. It is used on four evenings a week for out of school clubs.

The school child-centred ethos underpins the work of everyone in the school community at Hillside. This includes the vital work of cleaning, catering, clerical, technical and maintenance staff. Staff end-of-term meetings and any celebrations of success include all these people as a matter of course and there is clear recognition throughout the school of the importance of this wide teamwork.

And, of course, the curriculum continues to be developed and improved year-on-year and examination with results rising markedly since 2003, showing Hillside's absolute commitment to ensure all pupils achieve their potential. Hillside has shown remarkable progress and the children of 2012 achieve more than any other group before them even in the days of the Grammar School. It has been a long road to travel since 1910 with so many learners and teachers and support workers involved. The journey has been a success and the local community has been the winner.